To.
Mrs. John. Kellogg.
Allegan.
July 2. 1881. Michigan

presented by Miss Redpath
Cousin of the Author

Eng. by J. W. Watts from a Photograph by Grice Bros. Port au Prince.

Geffrard

A

GUIDE TO HAYTI.

EDITED BY

JAMES REDPATH.

BOSTON:
HAYTIAN BUREAU OF EMIGRATION,
221 WASHINGTON STREET.
[Tenth Thousand.] 1861.

STEREOTYPED AND PRINTED BY
GEO. C. RAND & AVERY.

DEDICATION.

TO

JAMES REDPATH, SENIOR,

OF ALLEGAN, MICHIGAN,

MY UNCLE,

AS A TESTIMONY OF GRATITUDE

FOR HIS

LONG AND UNWEARYING KINDNESS TO

MY FATHER'S FAMILY,

I DEDICATE THIS BOOK.

JAMES REDPATH.

Invitation.

Hayti will soon regain her ancient splendor. This marvellous soil that our fathers, bleſſed by God, conquered for us, will soon yield to us the wealth now hidden in its bosom. Let our black and yellow brethren, scattered through the Antilles, and North and South America, hasten to co-operate with us in reſtoring the glory of the Republic. Hayti is the common country of the black race. Our anceſtors, in taking poſſession of it, were careful to announce in the Conſtitution that they publiſhed, that all the descendants of Africans, and of the inhabitants of the Weſt Indies, belong by right to the Haytian family. The idea was grand and generous.

Liſten, then, all ye negroes and mulattoes who, in the vaſt Continent of America, suffer from the prejudices of caſte. The Republic calls you; she invites you to bring to her your arms and your minds. The regenerating work that she undertakes intereſts all colored people and their descendants, no matter what their origin, or where their place of birth.

Hayti, regaining her former position, retaking her ancient sceptre as Queen of the Antilles, will be a formal denial, most eloquent and peremptory, against those detractors of our race who contest our desire and ability to attain a high degree of civilization.

Geffrard.

Contents.

Book First — The Queen of the Antilles.

Book Second — The Republic and Emigration.

Book Third—Rough Notes and Essays.

Introduction.

THERE is only one country in the Western World where the Black and the man of color are undisputed lords; where the White is indebted for the liberty to live to the race which with us is enslaved; where neither laws, nor prejudices, nor historical memories, press cruelly on persons of African descent; where the people whom America degrades and drives from her are rulers, judges, and generals; men of extended commercial relations, authors, artists, and legislators; where the insolent question, so often asked with us, "What would become of the Negro if Slavery were abolished?" is answered by the fact of an independent Nationality of immovable stability, and a Government inspired with the spirit of progress. The name of this country is HAYTI. To Americans it presents an important and interesting study in whatever light regarded, —whether viewed, as the publicists of Europe regard the Union, as a new political experiment; or historically, as the home of a coming race, to be composed, like the English, by the mingling of various bloods; or philosophically, for the purpose of learning lessons for our own national guidance and instruction from the sanguinary chronicles of its wars of Independence. But it is to the friend of the Black, and, above all, to the enslaved and persecuted races in America, that Hayti presents the most important problem; to both it has a higher than a merely speculative interest; for to the philanthropist it suggests the thought of a duty to be performed, and to the proscribed it offers a home and a distinctive Nationality.

First interested in Hayti by the rare eloquence of Wendell Phillips, I sailed for Cape Haytian in January, 1859, for the purpose of describing the country and its people. During my voyage to the Island, a Revolution was successfully accomplished; an Emperor was banished, and a President installed. A new historical era had opened.

I remained in the Island two months, travelling on foot from Cape Haytian to Gonaïves; in an open boat from that town to Port-au-Prince, and on horseback from the capital to Jacmel. I occupied myself exclusively in gathering information, — geographical, political, and historical. I returned to Boston in April; but, finding that my Notes were incomplete, and in many instances contradictory, and desirous of correcting my first impressions by more extended studies, I again sailed for Hayti in June, — disembarking at Gonaïves; from which, in July, I made a pedestrian tour to the American colored settlement at L'Arcahaie. From that fertile district, I sailed to Port-au-Prince, where I resided until my departure in September.

My third visit was made in July of this year, for the purpose of exploring Tortuga and the other insular dependencies of Hayti.

In the mean time, among other patriotic projects of progress, material and moral, which the Government of President Geffrard had devised, was the plan of inviting an immigration into Hayti of all the enlightened and industrious men of African descent, in the States and the Provinces of North America. As an Abolitionist and a Republican, I felt a double interest in this project, — for not only will it be an agency of strengthening a colored Nation, by developing its resources, introducing new inventions, and bringing to it also moral sources of power, and thus demonstrating the capacity of the race for self-government, but it will carry out the programme of the ablest intellects of the Republican Party, — of surrounding the Southern States with a cordon of free labor, within which, like a scorpion girded by fire, Slavery must inevitably die. There is no country in the world better adapted for the culture of cotton, sugar, rice, and other Southern staples, than Hayti. All that it needs is laborers, intelligent and industrious, to devote themselves to the work. Thus, with the lever of an enlightened immigration in Hayti, the colored men of America could greatly aid in overturning the system of chattel Slavery in the South.

Brought into correspondence with the Government of Hayti, I suggested a number of guarantees to immigrants that should be officially announced; all of them, and many others subsequently asked for, (which will be found in the following pages) were immediately and publicly conceded. It will be found, also, that, in its desire for an enlightened immigration, the Government has transcended, not the demands only, but the expectations of the friends and representatives of the colored people in America. Requested to indicate the measures that should be employed to inform the class of immigrants invited of the nature of the country, the offers and intentions of the Government, and all the facts which men, seeking a new home, are naturally desirous of learning, I suggested, among other measures, the publication of a Guide Book, the establishment of a corresponding office in the States, and the appointment of Agents to visit the various localities in the Union and Canada in which there are settlements of men of African descent. This programme was adopted, and I was asked to take charge of its execution. I accepted the position, and prepared this book. The experience that I gained in the Kansas work had taught me that it is neither possible nor desirable to put into a Guide Book—for I once attempted to do so —all that intending emigrants will ask. Hence, in this volume, the reader will find the essential facts only; for further information, he must apply, personally or by letter, to the office in Boston, where certified copies of the Governmental guarantees, the journals of Hayti, books of reference, maps, specimens of the ores, and of the staple cultures of the Island, will be found.

All that section of this volume entitled "Official Part," is authorized by the Government of Hayti, having been submitted to the Minister of Exterior Relations, and other members of the Cabinet of President Geffrard. The original Documents bear the Seals of the respective Departments from which they emanated, or to which they were submitted for confirmation. For the rest, I have given my authorities, or write from my personal knowledge.

The Island of Hayti, originally divided between the French and Spanish, but reunited under President Boyer, in 1822, returned to its colonial political divisions in 1843, from causes which it would be entering into the domain of politics to enumerate. Since that time the Dominican Republic has held a large portion of the ancient Eastern or Spanish Part, and the Governments of Hayti the Western, or old French Part, with considerable annexations. As both Parts are nearly similar in their natural features, while writing in detail respecting Hayti, I have, at the same time, inserted a general geographical view of both of these Divisions.

The translations are by various hands; all of them are extremely literal. The Map accompanying the Geffrard Edition is the most accurate hitherto published.

JAMES REDPATH.

HAYTIAN BUREAU OF EMIGRATION,
No. 8 Washington Building, Boston.
December 3, 1860.

THE PINE AND PALM.

FANCY.

I.

On a bald peak Northern
  Stands the Pine-tree lonely:
Sleeping,—his white mantle
  Ice and snow-flakes only.

II.

Dreaming that a Palm-tree,
  Morning land adorning,
Lonely, on heights sultry,
  Silently is mourning.

H. Heine.

FACT.

I.

On the hills of Hayti,
  Wave the Palm-trees gladly:
Never in their slumbers
  Sigh the Pine-trees sadly.

II.

Verdant are their branches,
  Never winter-blighted;
Married,—see the loving
  Pines and Palms united.

Jas. Redpath.

Book First.

THE QUEEN OF THE ANTILLES.

HISTORY, GEOGRAPHY, NATURAL WEALTH.

I.

History of Hayti.*

IT was the 6th of December, 1492, that Christopher Columbus discovered the Island of Hayti. For this Caribbee name, the great navigator substituted that of Hispaniola, in honor of Spain, his adopted country.

It was the first land in America on which Europeans were to settle, and it was the first where the peaceful aborigines who inhabited it were to fall beneath the devouring activity of their new masters. The five caciques, who divided the authority, were subdued, some by the flattering manners of the Spaniards, and the rest by the force of their arms.

The brevity of this sketch forbids us to relate the many changes of the long drama which transformed this happy and populous island into a blood-stained desert. We refer those who are curious to learn this lamentable story, to the Life of Columbus, by Washington Irving. Suffice it to say, that the conquerors, having found quantities of gold in the country, abandoned themselves with eagerness to the research of this metal; and the aborigines, men little accustomed to labor, forced by their masters to the fatiguing work of the mines, quickly succumbed.

The discovery of the richer mines of Mexico caused those of

---

* Translated from the original sketch of Mr. Auguste Elie, of Port-au-Prince, which was written expressly for this volume.

Hayti to be abandoned, their working having become difficult on account of an insufficient population.

Another cause of decay was being developed at the same time. This was the war sustained by the Dutch, English, and French against the Spanish navigators, who designed to exclude every other flag from these new seas. These adventurers, who sailed in light vessels, and who afterwards became celebrated under the name of Buccaneers, settled at several points, and especially at Tortuga, a small island situated on the northern coast of Hayti. From thence, they spread by degrees over the main land, where they founded, under the protection of Cardinal Richelieu, the French colony of St. Domingo.

The Spaniards, from the commencement of their settlement, introduced slaves of African origin into Santo Domingo, the name of the capital, which, instead of Hispaniola, was soon applied to the whole island. The two oppressed races lived in the same tortures; but when, three centuries later, came the hour of deliverance, the public law of the new nationality recognized their common right to the exclusive property of the soil.

Under the Spanish dominion, the colony remained stationary. Three hundred years of possession had only produced a population varying from 100,000 to 150,000 souls.

The French had much greater success. In 1789, the portion which they possessed numbered a population of about 600,000, and five sixths of this population, compelled to labor in merciless bondage, had brought the property of the masters to the highest degree of prosperity.

The French Revolution now added another danger to that which had already shown itself in partial revolts amongst the slaves. The white colonists, and the free men of color* formed antagonistic parties, who discussed their privileges in presence of the trembling slave. The logical conclusion of such a state

* In Hayti, the phrase "men of color" is used exclusively to designate persons of mixed blood, black being applied and confined to those of pure African descent.

of things was necessarily the assertion of more general rights; and the insurrection of the slaves soon swept away all the institutions of the past. Slavery disappeared forever from the face of the country, and a decree of the National Convention legalized that universal liberty which had already become triumphant.

The colonists, from the commencement of the crisis, had partially pronounced in favor of deserting the cause of the Mother Country.

A few of the principal insurgent chiefs, especially Toussaint Louverture, soon began to think of independence. Their hatred of a past which they held in abhorrence prevented their alliance with any of the new parties. They passed from one flag to the very opposite one. Others, like Rigaud, devoted themselves to republican France; but the majority of them fought vigorously against the English, at that time the supporters of the slaveholders. In vain did Spain and England maintain the cause of the old *regime*. The newly freed, seconded by the energy of Sonthonax, member of the Convention, triumphed in the cause of liberty. In order to baffle the designs of independence entertained by Toussaint Louverture, and to establish the former state of things, Napoleon, First Consul, sent to St. Domingo an army composed of the soldiers of the Pyramids, Marengo, and Hohenlinden. One hundred and fifty millions of francs, and twenty thousand men of his best troops were swallowed up in this expedition, — one of the most terrible lessons ever read to this great man. The only gain accruing to him from this enterprise was the capture of Toussaint Louverture, (who was taken by treachery,) and the shame of the death of this celebrated chief, who perished of misery and cold in the Castle of Joux.

At the head of the valiant soldiers who had been fighting for ten years for their liberty, the most distinguished chiefs were Dessalines, Pétion, and Christophe. This time, it was no longer against servitude only that they unfurled their banner, — it was in the name of a higher principle, — that of National Independence.

The capitulation of the Cape, signed on the 28th of November, 1803, by General Rochambeau, was followed shortly after by the proclamation of independence. This act, which is the starting-point of Haytian nationality, was signed at Gonaïves on the 1st of January, 1804.

By the treaty of Bâle, Spain had abandoned to France the Spanish part of St. Domingo. Toussaint Louverture, in his capacity of governor-general, had gone to take possession of the country, and was there even at the time of the arrival of the French expedition. In the name of this right, in 1804, the Empire of Hayti was created, comprising the entire mainland, and the adjacent islands. Dessalines, named Emperor, sought to occupy Santo Domingo; but in this enterprise he failed, being baffled by the resistance of the inhabitants of the Eastern Part, who were supported by General Ferrand, commanding, in the name of France, a small remnant of the expedition of Napoleon.

The Constitution of 1804 was liberal. Its decrees have no longer any other than an historical interest. Nevertheless, one of its articles has survived its wreck, that, namely, on which is based the exceptional nationality of Hayti. It recognizes the right of property in the country to belong exclusively to men of the African or Indian races, and has been maintained in every subsequent Constitution.

Dessalines, on his accession as Emperor, was placed in a very embarrassing position, in a country entirely disorganized, and in which compulsory labor had always existed, even under Toussaint. In order to continue the traditions received from the past, he believed that, armed with dictatorial power, it was his duty to crush every obstacle that opposed his course. His cruelty arrayed against him his ancient companions in arms. Powerful enmities arose against him on all sides, and he was assassinated near Port-au-Prince, on his return from a journey to the Cape. This time a more liberal compact was adopted, in imitation of the Constitution of the United States. Christophe was called to the presidency of the Republic of Hayti, but the form of the new government being contrary to his wishes, he refused to accept its conditions, and began a fratricidal war, which lasted till his death.

Having failed in his attempt to seize Port-au-Prince, he withdrew to the Cape, which became the capital of the State of Hayti, and on the 2d of June, 1811, he caused himself to be crowned King. Endowed with talent for organization, but of a nature both despotic and cruel, he was unsuccessful in founding anything durable, for his artificial creations were unsupported by the aspirations of a free people. His attempts against the Republic, less powerful than his own State, failed on account of the secret support that Pétion found amongst the subjects of the King. At length, being unable, in consequence of an attack of paralysis, to mount his horse, when on the point of starting to repress a sedition, he blew out his brains on the 8th of October, 1820, in his palace of Sans Souci.

After the refusal of the presidency by Christophe in 1806. Pétion was named in his stead. An able statesman and a sincere republican, he had, during the whole course of his life, to struggle against men infinitely inferior to him in talent. Betrayed by his companions in arms, little understood even by men of note, he overcame by his address all the obstacles which appeared ready to crush him. His war against Christophe was his principal difficulty, but the secession of the Department of the South, which was, for a time, erected into an independent State under Rigaud, added, also, greatly to his embarrassments. This famous chief of the first wars of the Revolution, compromised his past glory in lending himself, at Cayes, to a division which might have proved fatal to the Republic.

After having reannexed the South, at the death of Rigaud, and repulsed an attack he sustained from Christophe, Pétion put into execution an idea which he had long before conceived.

He had understood, with his great sagacity, that, in order to settle the new society, it was necessary to attach to the soil, by ties of a nature agreeable to the existing institutions, those men who, for twenty years, as soldiers and civil officers, had served their country with devotion. He gave them, gratuitously, large quantities of land, and nearly all the territorial grants are dated from his time.

One of the objects of Pétion's attention was the Revision of the Constitution. In Hayti, the same fault had been committed as at Philadelphia; in presence of the Executive there had been created a Senate, invested with all the legislative power, as well as with some executive privileges. But with men less enlightened and less disciplined, the inconveniences of the system were still more disastrous. Profiting by acquired experience, Pétion demanded the Revision of the Constitution of 1806, and this was done at Grand Goâve, with all the legal forms, in the year 1816. This act, in its principal outline, was the result of an amalgamation of the American Constitution with the Constitution of the Year 3 of the French Republic.

Pétion died shortly after, worn out by twenty-five years of continual struggles. Posterity has been more just towards him than his contemporaries, and has placed him with reason at the head of the statesmen of his country.

General Boyer succeeded to the Presidency. He had the glory of repressing in the South the insurrection of a partisan chief, whom Pétion had never succeeded in subduing; of uniting, at the death of Christophe, the north of the Island to the Republic, and of effecting the annexation of the old Spanish Part to his dominions. Under his government of twenty-five years, the administration was put upon a better footing in all its branches, and the independence of the country recognized by the principal European Powers. But from the date of his treaty with France, in 1825, his vigor and activity were seen to diminish.* A kind of general languor spread over the Govern-

* Mr. Elie here refers to the Treaty, by which President Boyer agreed to pay

ment and the country, and this long peace was in no way utilized to the interest of the future. Boyer introduced paper money into the country. If he did not make a wrong use of this financial expedient, he was none the less its inventor; and the rate of the Spanish dollar fell sixty per cent. during his administration.

He was overthrown by a revolution set on foot by men of abilities much inferior to his own. He fell, struck down by a reaction of public opinion against him, provoked by an excess of vanity which blinded him to the fact that, though a man be superior in intellect to others, such superiority must be manifested in his actions. He believed that the power at his command would be sufficient to crush the pretensions of the opposition; but he was deceived.

He died in exile, which he bore with dignity, avoiding every step that might have been productive of agitation in his country. And the comparisons which have been made between his government and those that have succeeded it, have been wholly to his advantage.

Under the Provisional Government that succeeded him, a Constitution, resembling still more those of the United States than the preceding ones, was voted in due form. Only one of its articles was put into execution, viz: that which treated of the nomination of the President. General Herard Rivère, the leader of the last revolution, and a man of no note, sank, after a few months, overwhelmed by the reprobation of the public. This period is signalized by two important facts: the separation of the old Spanish Part from the Republic, and the insurrection of the mountaineers of the South. Fortunately the nomination of Guerier to the Presidency happened in time to extricate the country from the perilous position in which it was placed. Before this respected name, all parties laid down their arms. He

France one hundred and fifty millions of francs, for the recognition of Haytian Independence, and as an indemnity for the losses of the colonial proprietors. This treaty first created a national debt, and was very unpopular with the people.—ED.

took no further steps towards regaining possession of the old Spanish Part than the placing a corps of observation on the frontier, and the rest of the country was pacified.

Guerier died at the expiration of a year, after having restored to the country that tranquillity which had been disturbed during the last two years. His name is always mentioned, to this day, with expressions of national gratitude.

He was succeeded in power by General Pierrot, the brother-in-law of Christophe, a man utterly insignificant, and under whom the whole of the administration fell into great disorder. A military insurrection overthrew him, and called to the Presidency General Riché, a distinguished soldier.

The administration of Riché was short, but active and vigorous. A reform in several branches of the general administration was undertaken, and it is probable that if his early death had not arrested his progress he would have completely reorganized the public service. Having been one of Christophe's generals, he introduced into his government a severity which sometimes bordered on tyranny, but which was always in conformity with the principles of a strict discipline. Jealous of his power, like all the men of his school, he was pitiless towards the insurgents of the South, who reappeared at his accession.

The Constitution of 1844 had fallen during the events which separated the Spanish Part from the Republic, and threw, for a moment, (May, 1844,) the country into a state of complete anarchy. Guerier, possessing Dictatorial power, created a council of state invested with legislative powers and intrusted with the nomination of the President in case of vacancy. Pierrot governed the Republic in the same forms. On his accession to power, Riché adopted the Constitution of 1816, and instituted a senate which was to draw up a new fundamental pact. This was the origin of the constitutional law, which, with the exception of a few modifications introduced in 1859, still rules the country. It bears date the 15th November, 1846.

Riché died at the expiration of a year. General Faustin

Soulouque was elected by the Senate in his stead. He succeeded to power with the reputation of being a virtuous man, straightforward and well-disposed; but all parties soon discovered how greatly they had been deceived in him. Egotism and superstition were the springs of his actions, and the prolongation of his power tended to a complete disorganization of all administrative and social order. The revenue was publicly and unblushingly plundered, and the country was considered by the whole world as fast receding toward barbarism. Under the name of Faustin I., he caused himself to be crowned Emperor of Hayti; he had a court, a nobility, and all the ridiculous pageantry of the old monarchies. His cruelty rendered him odious, and his disrespect of individual rights made him utterly regardless of the feelings of persons of every class. The consuls of foreign Powers took toward his government a contemptuous attitude, which aided greatly in bringing it into disrepute.

This despotic power, which seemed so solid, fell at length, without resistance, by the breath of a man of courage,—the President of to-day. Accumulated hatred and ardent revenge clamored for the death of the Emperor, but the Government had the merit of protecting his embarkation. He withdrew to Jamaica, to fall again into the obscurity from which, for the happiness of mankind, he should never have issued.

The present Government, which has held for nearly two years the reins of administration, has above all applied itself to the healing of the wounds inflicted on the country by ten years of a fatal reign. It has touched on all questions of general interest, has succeeded in solving some, and is engaged in studying others. It understands that industry and agriculture are the first wants of a people settled on one of the richest soils in the world, and it goes forward with moderation, but with firmness, in the road of continuous improvement.

It has granted to the inhabitants of the Eastern Part a truce of five years, resolved to avoid a war which it is not for its interest to recommence; for it has enough to do to reörganize the interior and develop the resources it possesses. By persevering in these wise designs, it already occupies an honorable position among the Republics of the New World.

II.

Geography of Hayti.*

THE Island of Hayti, situated between 17° 55′ and 20° North latitude, and between the 68th and 75th degrees of West longitude from the meridian of Greenwich, is about 338 miles in length from East to West, whilst its breadth, from North to South, varies from 145 miles to 17; and its circumference, without including the bays, measures 848 miles. Its surface, exclusive of the adjacent islands, is estimated at 30,528 square miles †

The Island is situated at the entrance to the Gulf of Mexico, in the Atlantic Ocean. Itself one of the four great Antilles, it holds the next rank after Cuba, which is situated at a distance of 53 miles to the North-West. To the West South-West is situated Jamaica, at a distance of 109 miles; and 48 miles East South-East is the Island of Porto Rico. To the North, stretch Turk's Island and other headlands. To the South, Columbia is found at about 605 miles, and at a less distance are situated the Windward Islands. It may be said, therefore, that, of all the West India Islands, Hayti is the most advantageously situated with reference to the intercourse she may maintain with the surrounding isles and with Columbia, besides

*Translated from "La Géographie de l'Isle d'Haïti, par B. Ardouin: Port-au-Prince, réimprimée par T. Bouchereau, 1856." This is the volume in use in the schools of the Republic.

† That is to say: Hayti is about the size of Ireland.—Ed.

which, her communications with Europe and the United States only enhance this geographical position.

The adjacent islands belonging to Hayti are Gonave, Caïmites, Ile-à-Vaches, Béate, Alta Vela, Saône, St. Catharine, Mona, Monica, and La Tortue or Tortuga. We shall treat of each separately.

Hayti presents the appearance of a vast territory composed of mountains and plains.

"From the conformation of the surface of the Island," says M. de St. Méry, "which alternates in mountains and plains, arises a great variation in its climate and temperature. This is specially produced by the situation of the Island in the region of the trade winds, since the prevailing East wind, to the influence of which St. Domingo offers the whole of its length, makes for itself between the mountain chains many currents of air which refresh and temper these same mountains, — an advantage of which the plains do not partake, inasmuch as the mountains sometimes arrest the course of the wind, or change its direction. Moreover, a host of local circumstances, such as the elevation of the land, the quantity, more or less considerable, of water which irrigates the plains, the scarcity or abundance of forests, have a sensible influence on the character of the climate.

"If a powerful cause did not counterbalance the action of a scorching sun under the torrid zone, a sun which darts down its rays almost perpendicularly, during about three months of the year, upon St. Domingo, the temperature of this Island would be insupportable for man, or at least for such as were not designed by nature expressly as inhabitants of this climate. But this cause does exist in the wind of which we have just spoken, and whose salutary effects weaken those of the sun.

"To the protecting influence of the wind must be added the nearly equal length of the days and nights, and the abundant rains which produce constantly in the air a humidity at all times desirable, and which, bathing profusely the surface of the

Island, occasion, through the evaporation caused by the heat itself, a kind of cooling effect.

"Thus, by an immutable order, the contemplation of which enraptures the philosopher, nature has ordained that everything should aid in maintaining a sort of equilibrium in the climate of St. Domingo.

"The two seasons (summer and winter) are more marked in the mountains than in the plains, and in general the atmospheric changes are more frequent in the former. Here it is that the temperature is mildest, and here are never felt either the sultry heat or those winds which, when they become violent, are more apt to dry the air than to refresh and renew it.

"In fact, residence in the mountains is more pleasant than in the plains. Country life seems here to have a more simple character, and to be more independent of all those restraints which etiquette imposes as a law upon the towns, and even upon the neighboring country. It is seldom that the thermometer rises above 18 or 20 degrees,* whilst in the plains it reaches the mean rate of the towns, and consequently marks as high as 30 degrees.† The nights here are sometimes so cool that the use of a blanket is almost a necessity. There are even some mountains in St. Domingo where, at certain seasons, fire is a real enjoyment in the evening. This is not on account of any extreme cold, since the thermometer never sinks lower than about 12 or 14 degrees; ‡ but the contrast of this temperature to that of the day is so acutely felt that the words cold and heat are not to be understood in the same sense as in a cold climate."

Like the other West India Islands, Hayti is subject to the tempests which happen so often in this part of America, and which still bear the name given to them by the Indians. But it is the South part of the Island, including the country lying between Cape England and Iron Point, which suffers more

---

* Réaumur, equal to 72½ or 77 degrees, Fährenheit.
† Equal to 99½ degrees, Fährenheit.
‡ Equal to 59 or 63½ degrees, Fährenheit.

frequently than any other place from this destructive scourge. Nevertheless, M. de St. Méry has said, upon this subject: "The man who refers everything to himself, and who is exposed to the numberless evils which hurricanes may occasion, cannot easily discern their utility. But the philosopher, whom observation has convinced of the admirable order that governs the universe, takes for granted that they are useful, though he may not understand how, and rather than blaspheme against a cause so disastrous in appearance, he is willing to believe that these extraordinary movements of nature are necessary crises, in harmony with the principles whose workings secure the preservation of the globe, and that without them, perhaps, the Antilles would have been uninhabitable, on account of the incredible number of insects which cover the earth or flutter in the air."

Whatever may be the dangers of hurricanes, they cannot be compared in this respect to the earthquake. This dreadful phenomenon destroyed, in 1564, the town of Conception de la Vega, and has been felt more recently at Port-au-Prince, which was overthrown in 1770. Since this last epoch, shocks have taken place every year, but with much less intenseness. They are generally preceded by a deep noise, called in Hayti *goufre*, which is often heard without the shock being felt, and which is produced by a cause unknown as yet, but which appears to exist in the neighborhood of the lakes of Xaragua and Azuei, between Neybe and Port-au-Prince.

MOUNTAINS.

Several of these reach to a considerable elevation above the level of the sea. The principal range is that of *Cibao*, which forms a considerable group, almost in the centre of the Island, and from which diverge several chains in different directions. It rises to at least 7,673 feet perpendicular height, and is situated in the department of the North-East.

The *Selle*, the *Mexique*, and the *Bahoruco* or *Maniel* form the same chain which, after stretching from West to East, terminates in the South at the Point of Béate. The *Selle*, rising to the same height as the range of the Cibao, is situated about South East from Port-au-Prince, in the department of the West.

The *Hotte* comprises the chain which commences at the Platons, in the arrondissement of Cayes, crosses that of Grande Anse in the direction of East and West, and ends at Cap-à Foux, near Tiburon. Its height is also 7,673 English feet above the level of the sea.

The *Monte Christi* forms a chain which commences at Grange Point and ends at the Peninsula of Samana.

The mountains *Noire* and of *Cahos* begin near Marmelade, and terminate in the arrondissement of St. Jean.

Los Muertos form the chain which terminates at Cape Engaño, in the department of the South-East.

These last-named mountains, together with others less considerable, rise to an average height of about 2,400 feet.

"The number of mountains," says M. de St. Méry, "and their height, notwithstanding the vast extent of the several plains, give to the Island, when seen at a distance, a mountainous appearance, and is the reason why it is far from giving the favorable opinion it deserves. But the observer who contemplates the mountain chains with all their branches, which stretch their sinuous ramifications over the entire surface of the Island, sees in this the cause of its fertility, — the immense reservoir where are accumulated the waters which numberless rivers afterwards distribute on all sides; a means destined by nature to temper the effects of a burning sun, to arrest the fury of the winds, to vary the temperature, and even to multiply the resources and combinations of human industry; in short, the soil destined to bear for centuries the bounteous forests which, since the creation, perhaps, received the fertilizing waters which the clouds secrete within their bosom, and which, by their protective position, are saved from the touch of man, whose genius is not always conservative."

To these philosophic considerations, we may add the equally important observation which is naturally impressed upon the mind on viewing the mountains of Hayti, that these wild solitudes have been, and will ever be, the bulwarks of liberty and national independence.

PLAINS.

The most extensive plain in the Island, according to the same author, is that of *Vega Real*, situated in the department of the North-East. It extends over the arrondissements of Vega, San Yago, and Monte Christo. Its length is about 194 miles. It is remarkable for its fertility, and is watered by numerous rivers. Its principal production consists in tobacco, which is of excellent quality. Sugarcanes, cocoa, etc., are cultivated, and cattle are raised there, but its small population, scattered over so vast an extent of territory, is able to draw from this fruitful land only a small portion of these valued products. The river *Grand Yaque*, which discharges itself into the bays of Monte Christi, Mancenilla, and the *Youna*, which empties itself into the beautiful bay of Samana, will greatly facilitate the raising of these products, and will give to this superb plain a real importance when it possesses a larger and more active population.

From the left hand of the Ozama to the Cape Engaño, there stretches an extent of land about 145 miles long, measuring 4096 square miles, of which more than 3,500 are plains; this is also watered by several rivers. The produce raised comprises sugar, coffee, tobacco, mahogany, horned cattle, and other animals. Its soil is very fertile.

The plain of *Azua*, which includes the space between the river Neybe and the bay of Caldera, covers a surface of 879 square miles. It has a soil of astonishing fertility, notwithstanding the drought which usually prevails. Here very fine sugar is made, and the rearing of cattle and the cutting of mahogany form also branches of industry, as throughout the whole of the Eastern part of the Island.

The plain of *Neybe* measures 469 square miles, and yields the same kind of produce as that of Azua.

The lowlands, situated at the foot of the *Bahoruco*, to the East and West, comprise an extent of surface measuring 820 square miles. They would offer the same advantages if cultivated.

The plains of *St. Jean*, of *Banica*, and of *Hinche*, called the valleys of *St. Thomas* and *Goave*, cover a surface of 1172 square miles. The cattle raised in these rich pasture lands form the principal branch of industry for the inhabitants of these parts, who have much increased since 1822. All the other products of the country are also easily obtained.

The plains of the *North*, starting from the river of *Massacre* as far as the limits of Port Margot, may be estimated as covering, all together, a superficies of 1055 square miles. The sugar-cane is here advantageously cultivated.

The plain of *Cul de Sac*, near Port-au-Prince, measures 20 miles from East to West, while its breadth, from North to South, varies from 6 miles to 10. It was not until 1724 that the sugarcane was here planted. The usual aridity of this plain forced the inhabitants to resort to the irrigation of this precious plant in 1730; and the effects of this powerful natural agent were such that before the Revolution, about fifty million pounds of this article were produced. This immense result is no longer obtained.

The plain of *Gonaïves* may be estimated at 141 square miles in extent. It yields principally a cotton which is highly valued.

That of the *Artibonite*, which is watered by the river of this name, and by many other smaller ones, appears to have been formed by deposits from these rivers, since, at a depth of 30 feet, there have been found different beds, in which have been discovered leaves and branches of trees. Sugar and cotton are grown here. Its surface is supposed to cover about 263 square miles.

That of *Arcahaie*, situated like an amphitheatre along the seaboard, extends about 12 miles from East to West, by about 1800 feet in its greatest breadth, from North to South. The sugar here produced is of excellent quality, though the quantity is small.

The plain of *Léogane* measures about 17 miles in its greatest length from East to West, and scarcely 7 miles in breadth from North to South. It yields sugar of great beauty.

Finally, that of *Cayes* offers a surface of about 117 square miles. Here, as in the plain of Cul de Sac, the different streams are usefully employed in watering the sugarcane,—a production which offers such considerable reward to the laborious workmen.

RIVERS.

Few countries are as well watered as Hayti. This advantage is owing, as we have already seen, to the mountains which feed the numerous rivers that nature has spread over all this fortunate Island. But the departments of the East are much more favored, in this respect, than the others, and other rivers are also much more considerable.

The longest river is the *Artibonite*, which the Indians called *Hatibonico.* Its entire length is 145 miles. It flows in a straight line from the Cibao, where it rises. Before it reaches this sea, its volume is increased by a multitude of other rivers, such as the *Guayamuco*, the *Rio Canas*, the *Fer-a-Cheval*, etc. It frequently inundates the plain which bears its name, and by this means produces the same effect as the Nile in Egypt.

The other principal rivers are the *Yuna* and the great *Yaque*, in the department of the North-East; the *Ozama*, the *Isabela*, the *Macoris*, the *Soco*, the *Quiabon*, the *Romana*, the *Jayna*, the little *Yaque*, and the *Neyba*, in the department of the South-East; the rivers of *Cayes*, *Cavaillon*, *Jérémie*, and *Nippes*, in the department of the South; those of *Jacmel*, *Léogane*, and *Cul de Sac*, in the department of the West; and the *Massacre*, the *Grande Riviere*, and the *Trois-Rivieres*, in the department of the North.

MINERAL WATERS.

The number of mineral springs which exist over all the surface of Hayti is another of its many riches.

The principal one is that of *Port-à-Piment*, in the department of the Artibonite, formerly called *Eaux de Boynes*, (waters of Boynes,) but which at present might be more properly styled *Eaux de Capoix*, (waters of Capoix,) in order to make amends for the injustice committed towards their discoverer, — an injustice against which M. de St. Méry has so loudly exclaimed, attributing to flattery the denomination these waters obtained. Before the Revolution, considerable establishments were here made, but they do not now exist. It would be highly desirable to see them again established, and under the direction of a skilful physician, who might superintend the treatment of the sick persons who have often recourse to these springs. Many diseases which the faculty have pronounced incurable, have here met with a complete cure. Seven springs are here grouped together in the same spot.

The same properties have been discovered in the springs of *Banica*, situated five miles distant from the town, and in the same department. There are four in this place, which is equally deprived of suitable establishments.

Other minor springs exist in the communes of Dalmarie, Irois, Tiburon, Jacmel, Mirebalais, etc.

LAKES.

The largest is the *Etang Salé*, (salt lake,) called, also, the lake of *Xaragua* and *Henriquille*, because the Cacique Henri, with his followers, took refuge here upon a small island situated in the centre of the lake, and measuring 5 miles in length by 2½ in breadth. This Island is peopled with wild goats. The Etang Salé, situated in the department of the West, is about 22 miles long and 8½ broad; and is about 53 miles in circumference. It is deep, and swarms with alligators. The water is clear, but bitter salt, and has a disagreeable odor, and ebbs and flows like the sea.

About five miles North-West from this lake is found another, running in the same direction, but measuring only 12 miles long, and in breadth varying from $2\frac{1}{2}$ to 7 miles. It is called the *Etang Saumâtre*, on account of the acrid taste of its waters, or *Laguna de Azuei*. This lake also has its tides.

To the South of the Etang Salé, at $2\frac{1}{2}$ miles' distance, lies the *Etang Doux*, (sweet lake,) named also *Laguna Icotea*, (the lake of turtles,) which is nearly 5 miles long by $1\frac{1}{8}$ miles broad. This lake has no communication with the other two, and its extent depends upon the rains and the floods which maintain it. It abounds in turtle, good fish, and sea-fowl.

The lake of *Miragoâne*, in the department of the South, is 7 miles long by 12,000 feet broad. Its circuit, counting the indentations, is supposed to measure 17 miles. Its depth averages 180 feet. Its waters flow into the sea at the Acul du Carénage, near the town of Miragoâne, and are used by the inhabitants. This lake is crossed by a wooden bridge, with stone abutments, on the road from Petit-Goâve to Miragoâne. The intention was formerly entertained of constructing a canal between the *Acul du Petit-Goâve* and this lake for the transport of provisions and produce.

The project was also formed of digging a canal between the Etang Saumâtre and the *embarcadère du fossé*, near the town of Port-au-Prince. This canal would thus have traversed the plain of *Cul de Sac* in all its length, and would have served to convey the immense quantity of sugar here made. In 1822, government caused to be built upon this lake, and upon the Etang Salé, a barge and lights, in order to facilitate the communications of the capital with the department of the South-East, and to spare travellers a painful journey by a road cut through the rocks on the north bank of the Etang Saumâtre. But the force of habit prevents people profiting by these facilities. It is true that the service of these boats is much neglected by the sailors appointed to them, and that a great and often insurmountable difficulty prevails almost always in these lakes; this is the violence with which the East and West winds blow between the mountains that surround the lakes.

This difficulty might be removed by the establishment of steamboats, which would possess the twofold advantage of facilitating intercourse and of helping in the conveyance of cattle from Neybe and Azua to the plain of the Cul-de-Sac. But these ameliorations can only be the work of time; they will no doubt come with the increase of the population, which serves in all countries to develop industry.

BAYS.

The largest and the most beautiful bay of Hayti is that of *Samana.* It is situated between capes Samana and Raphaël. Christopher Columbus called it *Baie des Flèches,* (bay of arrows,) because he found on its shores large numbers of Indians armed with arrows. The distance between its two extreme capes is 17 miles. It has an average breadth of 12 miles, and is about 50 miles in depth. The most powerful squadrons could find in it a sure asylum; but the channel by which it is entered is difficult and narrow. A vessel must pass under the cannon of the fort *Cacao,* built since 1822. The extent of this magnificent bay, its position on the windward side of the Island, together with the immense quantity of wood found in the peninsula, fit for naval purposes, and the mines of iron and copper concealed within its bosom, — all these advantages tend to make the point the most important of all in a maritime point of view. Whale-fishery might here be carried on.

The other bays, whose importance and extent differ more or less, are those of *Môle St. Nicolas, Ocoa, Higuey, Neybe, Jacmel, Bainet, Flamands, Mesle, St. Louis, Caïmites, Baradères, Miragoâne, Petit-Goâve, Port-au-Prince, St. Marc, Gonaïves, Henne, Acul du Nord, Caracol, Fort Liberté, Mancenille, Monte Christi,* and the *Baie Ecossaise.*

CAPES.

The coasts of the Island present the following promontories, namely:

The former Cape Français, Cape Cabron, Cape Samana, in the department of the North-East; the capes Raphaël, Engaño, Espada, in the department of the South-East; the *Faux Cape*, Capes Mongon, Jacmel, Bainet, and St. Marc, in the department of the West; Cape Tiburon, Cap-a-Foux, and Cape Dalmarie, in the department of the South; and Cap-a-Foux and Cape St. Nicolas in the department of the Artibonite.

PENINSULAS.

Hayti contains three: that of Samana, which is the most important; that of Mole St. Nicolas, and that of Baradères. The first is 36 miles long from East to West, with a breadth which varies from 12 miles to 5. It is covered almost entirely with mountains, and is watered by more than twenty rivers. The second extends, in a straight line, a distance of 19,200 feet by 7,800 in breadth. That of Baradères, called more frequently *Bec du Marsouin*, is 5 miles long South-West and North-East, by a breadth which varies from 2,250 to 9,000 feet. It abounds in fine wood, suitable for building, and, at the commencement of the year, fishermen here assemble for the great fisheries, which supply salted fish for home consumption, similar to that found on the shores of Gonave. The *Bec du Marsouin* is 18° 33′ 40″ latitude North, and 73° 35′ 5″ longitude West, at the eastern point.

ADJACENT ISLANDS.

Gonave. This Island, situated at the entrance of the small gulf which fills up the space between Cape St. Nicolas and Cape Dalmarie, is 35 miles in length, and 8½ in its greatest breadth. It is the largest of all the islands which border on Hayti and are under its dependence. There is at the centre of the Gonave a lake of considerable size, and the springs found here appear to be infiltrations. The air is healthy. It contains wood fit for building purposes.

At the time of the murder of the court of the Queen *Anacoana*, many Indians took refuge here. They named it *Guanabo* or *Guanavaux*, which has been corrupted to Gonave. The eastern point of this Island is 18° 42′ 30″ North latitude, and 72° 53′ 11″ West longitude; the western point, 18° 52′ 40″ latitude, and 73° 24′ 11″ longitude.

La Tortue, [*Tortuga*,] situated at a short distance from the Northern coast, opposite Port de Paix, is 22 miles long and 18,000 feet in average breadth. Its superficies is of 11,734 carreaux, (3 acres make a carreau.) This is the spot where the Buccaneers first settled in 1630; and in 1694, it was abandoned for the establishments which had been made on the main land. This Island also abounds in very fine timber; here is found a kind of red crab, highly prized by amateurs, who do not appear to dread its effects, although the manchineel tree is known to grow at La Tortue. The centre of this Island is in latitude 20° 4′.

La Saône. This Island, situated to the windward of Santo Domingo, quite near the Bay of Higuey, is about 19 miles long from East to West, and 5 broad from North to South, and nearly 62 miles in circumference. It is very fertile; the Indians called it *Adamanoy*. A cacique lived here, who was sovereign of the Island, and independent of those who reigned in Hayti. The Spaniards had this cacique devoured by a dog; this atrocious act brought on a war between them and the Indians, in which the latter were all sacrificed. After the perpetration of these cruelties, sugarcane was grown there by the Africans, whom the Spaniards had introduced; but from a remote period, it has not been inhabited.

St. Catharine. This Island, so called after the name of its proprietor, (a lady,) is situated to the leeward of the Saône, opposite the River *Romana*. Its extent is small, but it is covered with abundance of game; it was formerly cultivated.

La Béate is situated at a distance of about 18,000 feet to the S. W. of the point of Béate or Bahoruco. It is 6 miles in length from East to West, and scarcely 5 miles in average breadth. Formerly it contained plantations and cattle pens; it abounds in game. Christopher Columbus landed here in 1504. A few years ago it was used as a place of refuge by the pirates who infested that Caribbean Sea. Its centre is in latitude 17° 51′ and longitude 71° 40′ 38″.

Alta-Vela, thus named by Columbus in 1494, is 5 miles S. S. W. of *La Béate*. It is 90,000 feet in its greatest length, and as much in its broadest part. It contains excellent timber.

L'île-à-Vaches. This Island is situated about 7 miles S. S. E. of the town of Cayes, and measures 10 miles in length, and rather more than 2½ in breadth. It derives its name, which it received from the Buccaneers, from the large number of cows found there. It has often been used by pirates as a harbor of refuge. The East Point is 18° 3′ latitude, and 73° 29′ 58″ longitude, and the Northwesterly Point 18° 6′ 10″ latitude, and 73° 47′ 43″ longitude.

The *Caïmites*. These are small islands, the largest of which covers a surface of about two square leagues; they are situated to the N. W. of the Peninsula of Baradères, opposite Corail and Pestel. They yield very fine timber.

Mona and *Monica* are two small islands, situated to the East of Saône, between Hayti and Porto Rico. Mona is fully two leagues from East to West, and rather more from North to South. It has two harbors capable of holding moderate-sized vessels, and everything necessary to cultivation and cattle rearing. In 1512 it was given to Bartholomew Columbus by the king of Spain. It was then highly cultivated and yielded a large revenue to its proprietors. But it appears to have been deserted long ago.

Monica is smaller than the preceding island.

Navazo, a small guano island, situated between Hayti and Jamaica, is the only other dependency.

III.

The Animal Kingdom.

HAYTI, when discovered, contained very few animals, and of these one species only remains, the agouti, a rare and inoffensive creature about the size of a rabbit.

DOMESTIC ANIMALS.

All of our domestic animals are abundant. The horses are small, but of great endurance; resembling, in both of these respects, our Indian ponies. They are never shod. They are of the Andalusian breed, spirited, swift, require little care, and have a fine gait. Those belonging to the lower class are lean, shaggy, and never groomed. From $700 to $1,000, Haytian, is the average price for a good horse in the country; but in the towns they ask much higher; sometimes, but rarely, very fine horses sell at from $4,000 to $5,000. Emigrants should bring out their own harness, as the Haytians generally use ropes only, made out of the bark of the cocoa-tree and other vegetables substances. If the emigrant buys saddles, he should remember that they must be fit for ponies, — not large horses. Asses and mules, which are the chief carriers in the country, are very common and cheap. Asses, from $100 to $400, Haytian; mules from $500 to $2,000, Haytian. Hogs are lean, and active; their flesh is said to be good; it is never cured, but sometimes dried in the sun; the race requires to be crossed with fatter breeds. Wild hogs abound in certain districts. Oxen, also, are small, and lean; they are much used in the interior for drawing; their flesh, in consequence of poor feed and bad slaughtering, is often dry and tough, as compared with American beef. Emigrants should bring yokes with them; as the "habitans" of Hayti use ropes, tied to the horns or to a straight stick, — the usual method of the West Indies, — which requires ten oxen to do what one could easily perform. The cows give good milk; but very little cheese and butter is made. These are imported from the States. Emigrants should stop this trade by bringing churns with them. Calves are rarely killed. It requires an order from the police officers to kill beef-cattle, sheep, or hogs. This law prevents theft. Sheep flourish, and their flesh is delicious when properly slaughtered. They are never sheared, although their wool, when they are young, is of fine quality. In consequence of this negligence a lucrative commerce is lost; the creature suffers; and the fine wool gives place to a long, coarse hair, as soon as the animal attains its full growth. Goats prosper, and their milk is generally used, and their flesh eaten. At Furcy,* about 20 miles from Port-au-Prince,— where there are forests of pine trees and other woods and vegetables of the temperate zones, — a friend of the editor recently purchased a goat for a Spanish dollar. Dogs and cats would soon become extinct, if not kept up by the introduction of foreign breeds. Rats and mice are found; hares and rabbits are rare. It is probable that emigrants might profitably introduce various breeds of the different domestic animals with advantage to themselves and the country.

BIRDS.

All kinds of poultry known in the States are common in Hayti; the flesh of the turkey is particularly delicious. As it costs nothing in the country to keep poultry, and as they not only do not injure any of the staples, but destroy the mischievous cockroach and other obnoxious insects, it would be

* At this place the Government have established a model farm. The thermometer there ranges thus, 58° (Fährenheit) at early morning; 78° noon; 61° in the evening, in the hot months of July and August.

well for the emigrant to establish a poultry yard at once. Birds are numerous, but singers are rare. Among the more common of the feathered creation in Hayti, are green parrots, parroquets, nightingales, mocking-birds, humming-birds, tropic-birds, musicians, swallows, turtle doves, woodpeckers, pelicans, kingfishers, flamingoes, cardinals, partridges, wild geese, wild pigeons, wild ducks, ortolans, boobies, snipes, man-of-war birds, crab-eaters, bullfinches, aigrets, *gris-gris*, white owls, brown owls, *collier*, and hawks.

FISHES.

Fish abound in the rivers and lakes and along the coasts of Hayti. There is a great variety of excellent fish for consumption. Sharks frequent the harbors. Among the more common fish are mullets, gray and red sardans, sardines, dolphins, carps, bonitoes, pikes, doradoes, gurnets, hammer-heads, garfish, porpoises, brills, eels, bull-heads, sea-cows, tunny-fish, sword-fish, flying-fish, sun-fish, *caranque*, *vivanneau*, *bécune*, *cayeux*, *barbarin*, *tasard*, *souffleur*, *pisquet*, sea-anemones. Common crabs, Moorish crabs, gallo-crabs, lobsters, and shrimps are plentiful. Oysters are found in great numbers along the coasts, clinging to the mango bushes, that grow in large groves in every part of the sea-shore. They are of small size, and are said to be of good flavor. There are various varieties of shell-fish, including conches, periwinkles, pearl-oysters, burgan, lambi, sea-urchins, murex, helmet-shell, *vis*, *ducal*, *music*, *soudon*, and *palourde*. There are many reefs where coral of exquisite beauty may be gathered, as also polypi and sponges.

INSECTS.

Insects are plentiful in all tropical climates, and Hayti forms no exception to the rule. We can notice a very few only. Among the poisonous insects are the scorpion, centipedes, and three kind of spiders. The bite of none of them is mortal, or even dangerous, if the ordinary remedy is taken in due time. The bite of these insects causes inflammation; the remedy is alkali, in fluid form, applied to the wound, and five drops dissolved in water to be drunk. Wild bees are numerous, and their wax and honey are sometimes exported. Before using the honey, however, the emigrants should first learn from the natives how to distinguish that which is made from the poisonous plants. There is a great variety of butterflies. The fireflies are exceedingly brilliant. Cockroaches, ants, caterpillars, grasshoppers, mosquitoes, wasps, locusts, moths, sand-flies, fleas, bugs, lice, weevils, chiques, and ticks, and other members of the same family, will also be found in every part of the Island. Mosquitoes are as noisy, but not so annoying as their American compatriots. Cockroaches and ants are the greatest pests to housekeepers; they eat clothing and books with an extraordinary gluttony.

REPTILES.

Of the reptiles, the lizard is the most common; there is every variety of them, but all of them are innoxious. Alligators and caymans are occasionally seen in the rivers. Frogs and toads are numerous. Turtles are counted by the million. The serpent family is rarely met with; there are but very few snakes, and they are not venomous. The most beautiful of the native snakes is the magdalena.

IV.

The Vegetable Kingdom.

AN inhabitant of the temperate zones can hardly conceive how rich Hayti is in every species of vegetable wealth. She has every tree and fruit and flower of the tropics in her plains; and there is nothing that grows in the States or in Canada, that cannot be successfully cultivated on her highlands. Land alike of the pine and the palm, of the bread-fruit and the strawberry, of the gigantic cactus and the lowly violet, for richness of verdure and variety of vegetable products, Hayti is not excelled — perhaps not equalled — by any other country in the world. Folio volumes have been written on her flora; but the briefest notes must suffice us here.

STAPLES.

Cotton grows with extraordinary facility, requiring no culture whatever. It is of a fine and silky quality. It does not grow on bushes, but trees, which produce two crops annually and last several years. Its culture might be made exceedingly profitable, as no country is better adapted for its growth.

Coffee flourishes on the highlands. The principal crop is gathered in December and January; but in May there is a second crop called "grapillage." If properly cultivated,— one plant for every ten feet, or 1,225 bushes per carreau,—reckoning four pounds from each tree annually, (the minimum result,) every carreau would thus produce 4,900 pounds of coffee. This crop, sold at the annual average rate of 125 gourdes per 100 lbs., would produce a revenue of 6,125 gourdes, or $471 per annum. As the Republic will give five carreaux of land to each family of emigrants, the revenue thus placed within the reach of every industrious man, of African descent, after a residence of two or three years, may easily be estimated by them.

Sugarcane is a native of the plains, where the traveller often sees, with astonishment, gigantic specimens of it, varying from 18 to 24 feet in height. Mr. Devimeux, a planter of Port-au-Prince, three years ago, exhibited a cane five inches in diameter. Once planted, this staple requires no further care, excepting to be cut down when it reaches maturity. As soon as cut, it begins to sprout again; and for at least ten years no replanting is necessary. A carreau of land, planted with cane, will produce, on an average, 9,000 lbs. of raw sugar.

Cocoa grows in the valleys, on trees, and requires little attention. It is a profitable and important article of export.

Rice, of good quality, is cultivated with success, but hitherto on a limited scale.

Tobacco, with similar advantages of production, is treated with a similar neglect. Hayti, in times past, has produced tobacco equal in quality to that of Cuba; and it is to be hoped that she will soon again enter into competition with her slaveholding neighbor in this culture.

Indian corn grows everywhere, and brings good prices in the markets. Emigrants would do well in introducing the seeds of the finest varieties.

Ginger is produced in great abundance, and might be made an important export.

Indigo grows everywhere spontaneously, and was largely exported in the time of the French. It gives two crops a year. No produce, for an equal volume, returns so great a profit. Without intrenching on the other staples, the Republic could furnish two millions of dollars' worth of indigo per annum.

Manioc is exceeding productive; and, rightly cultivated, would yield an immense revenue. It is easily raised, even on the mountains, but it flourishes best on the plains. Cassava bread is manufactured from its root; but a more lucrative use of it would be to make starch.

The Palmi-Christi, (from the berries of which castor-oil is drawn,) pepper and pimentum, need rather more care to gather than to plant; for immense quantities are annually lost for the want of hands to collect their products.

Oranges, citrons, mangoes, bananas, plantains, pineapples, and other fruits must suffer the same fate, until a line of steamships is started between the Republic and the United States,—a measure which is in contemplation by the Government of Hayti.

Arrowroot could be cultivated with great profit and success; but at present it is almost entirely neglected.

VEGETABLES AND FRUITS FOR HOME CONSUMPTION.

We have said that everything that grows in the States and the Canadas can be raised in Hayti; but not necessarily in every part of it.

Clover, cabbages, and potatoes, for example, do not flourish in the plains, although they are abundantly productive in the highlands. The plains bear the fruits and trees of the tropics; while the mountains yield coffee and all the productions of the temperate zones. Among the vegetables and fruits that are used for home consumption only, are plantains, bananas, cocoanuts, sweet potatoes, Irish potatoes, yams, artichokes, egg-plants, mangoes, oranges, asparagus, bread-fruit, vegetable-butter, *(laurus persea,* in Creole, *avocate,)* vegetable-soap, *(sapindus sapponaria,)* apples, pineapples, strawberries, blackberries, mulberries, peaches, grapes, carrots, cabbages, radishes, pumpkins, beets, onions, celery, mint, parsley, and turnips.

FRUITS FOR PRESERVES, AND FLOWERS FOR PERFUMES.

Sugar refineries once more reëstablished, a large trade would necessarily arise in preserved fruits for exportation. The high price paid for white sugar at present prevents this branch of commerce from flourishing. Oranges, lemons, figs, guavas, apricots of the Antilles, (*class xiii. Polyandrie monogymie*, Lin.,) pineapples of every variety, pomegranates, shaddocks, mangoes, rose-apples, custard-apples, cachimants, caïmites, (*Chrysophyllum caïmit*, Lin.,) papaws, sapodillas, dates, avocates, and the other luscious fruits of the tropics, — all of which are to be found in Hayti,—would furnish unfailing and abundant sources of wealth in this department of industry.

Another lucrative commerce, awaiting development, is that of extracting perfumes from flowers. Thousands of frangy-panni, jasmines, vervaines,—all the innumerable flowers of the tropics, — now literally waste their sweet perfumes on the desert air, for the want of a proper knowledge of the methods of saving them. There are no fine essences and perfumes sold in the civilized world that could not be manufactured in Hayti.

MEDICAL PLANTS.

It is asserted by scientific men, that the flora of Hayti — only partly explored by Tussac, Descourtilz, and others — contains still many secrets which, if known, would render invaluable aid to the medical art. For, medicinal plants abound everywhere; and everything that is brought, for pharmaceutic purposes, from Africa and South America, is to be found on this Island. Our space permits only a verbal enumeration of some of the principal medicinal plants. There are:

Aloës, balsam copaiva, wild-cinnamon tree, tannin, mint, sage, wild sage, quinquina, all the kinds of acacias, ricinoïdes, cascarillas, vanilla, myrth, absinth, valériane, mélisse, rosemary, camphor-tree, cloves, nutmegs, shrub trefoïl, quassias, jesuits-powder, gentian centaury, menyanthes, indian arbro-boot, wood-sorrel, swallow apple, false sycamore, purstane, jerusalem oak, fern-polypody, cactus grandiflorus, divaricatus, flagelliformis, laurel-tree, cinomorium, coccineum, ipecacuanha, euphorbia myrtifolia, ticassia, tamarin royoc, rhubarb, senna, hop-bryony, jalap, marchantia chenopoda, dodder, negro conhaye, costus, indian cane, long-rooted birthwort, cuete, winter-cherry, yellow-iris, passion-flower, wall-pellitory, cookia-wampi, sapindus saponaria, sesamum orientale, jujube-tree, sebesten, gerard, pittes, squil, venus-hair, peresky lautana camara, black nightshade, vitis labrusca, inga, gomphrœna globosa, euphoria punicea, monbin, couroupita guyanensis, spanish-plum, begonia litida, theophrasta americana minat., laurus camphora, capparis cynophallophora, misseltoe, locust-tree, peruvian balsam-tree, lime-tree, croton corylifolium, monarda coccinea, passiflora fœtida, pitton, solanum quitœnse, argemona mexicana, purslane, hibiscus trilobus, semson, loranthus americanus, vervain, lecythis grandiflora, pharus lappulaceus sida americana, isora, elais guineensis, cedrela odorata, boar-tree, fagara guianensis, spetted navel estail, cactus fimbriatus, euphorbium, areca, piper aromaticum, piper discolor, uvaria arom. zeylanica, cubebs-shrub, mustard, fustic-wood, myristica sebifera, urtica baccifera, crotalaria sagittalis, stœchas amer. lato serratogne folio, iron wood, epidendrum obtusifol., epidendrum candatum, cordia collococca, cassia alata, vateirca guian., maple-leaved liquidamber, ballota odorata, sago-tree, palma humilis coccifera latifolia mayor, holly, india-rubber tree, juglans, fraxinifolia, ferolia variegata, smilax salsaparilla, guyacum, Chinese smilax, sassafras-tree, lobea syphilitica, ovieda spinosa, toluifera balsamum, copaiba-tree offic., croton origanifol., cissus sisyoides, heliotropium indicum, hemp agrimony, aspalatus ebenus, pistia stratiotes fol. obcord., cinchona nitida, caryota urens, cactus monoliformis, cactus nobilis, cactus cochenillefer, cactus triangul., bread-nuts, artocarpus incisa, indian arrowroot, theyreat bean, cinnamon-tree, panax quiquefol., tubera candida, henbane, white water-lily, laurus persea, anagyris, welted frajeles, common feverfew, hypoxis scorzonera, broad-leaved-egyptian privet, nymphæa lotus, nelumbo indica, camomile.

POISONOUS PLANTS.

All tropical countries produce poisonous plants; but as they are easily recognized they seldom injure. Emigrants should eat no fruits until they know what they are. In Hayti, there are three kinds of fruits, all poisonous, of the mancinella-tree, which somewhat resemble the citron, and thereby deceive children. But, as the tree is always destroyed as soon as it is discovered, it is extremely rare. The chief poisonous plants of Hayti are : —

Poisoned hog-meat, (aristolochia arborescens,) snake-nut, gouaré, cestrum nocturnum, tree arum, (three different kinds,) trefoil-leaved dragon, cissus caustica, dolichos obtusifolius, dolichos minimus, thorn-apple, deadly nightshade, goats-rue, amaryllis punicea, black nightshade, milky dogsbane, and cissampelos.

WOODS.

Comparatively — considering its extent and fertility — unpeopled, Hayti has vast tracts of forest lands, many of which have never been exploited for sixty years, and abound therefore in every variety of wood for building, cabinet-making, ship-architecture, dyeing, and tanning. The chief woods exploited are mahogany and logwood; and these, too, are taken from the most easily accessible places only, and without any aid from the appliances of modern art. The coasts, the banks of the Artibonite and other rivers furnish all the woods at present exported, but the exhaustless forests elsewhere, which it would not be difficult to work, remain still in their primitive condition. For house-building the Island furnishes magnificent pines, and a species of an oak (Bignonia guercus) as firm as that of Europe, and impervious to worms. For frame and joint work, anacardium occidentale furnishes a good white wood; and for pile-work, there is the acacia mimom. tenuifolia, which lasts for a century. For ship-building, the oak, iron-woods, auzuba fructu glutinosa and the ácomas, (which furnish masts 60 feet long and 18 inches in diameter,) as well as the pines, already mentioned, and other hard woods. For cabinet-making, mahogany of every variety, (the best in all the world,) ebony, lancewood, ferolia variegato, red and yellow satinwood, abound and are capable of receiving a high polish; as also, are the zanthoxylum caribæum, which is likewise a dye-wood, the erithalis fruticosa, which preserves its fine odor, orange-wood, rose-wood, guyacum, laurus, sassafras, and different kinds of the walnut. Among the dye-woods are, logwood, in quantities inexhaustible, fustic, and satin-wood, (yellow;). Brazilwood, (carmine;) myrthus cotenifolia, (yellow and brown;) laurus sassafras, (yellow;) colocoba uvifera, (red;) Braziliastrum americanum, (brownish red;) malphigia urens, (red and black;) morus tinctoria, (yellow;) and the roots of laurus jasmini folio, a sort of iron-wood, which give a violet dye. There are hundreds of others which it is impossible to enumerate. For tanning purposes there are many trees whose bark is invaluable, — such as the guava, corossol, anona squamosa, cupana americana, malphigia specata, and innumerable hosts of others. For paper manufacturing, now that there is so great a demand for materials, Hayti might export an inexhaustible supply of aloes, perfoliata, and other plants which serve to make good common paper. Of resinous woods there is a great variety.

V.

The Mineral Kingdom.*

THE existence of immense mineral riches in the Island of Hayti is too well substantiated to require any argument to prove it. Its possessions of metallic ores were the first that stimulated European cupidity soon after the discovery of the Western World. Several of these mines, in the Eastern section of the Island, have been imperfectly worked in times past, but the age was not then sufficiently advanced in scientific knowledge, to have been acquainted with the means and appliances necessary for their successful exploration. In Hayti, proper, the mineral wealth of the country has been yet still more neglected. Their exploration has hitherto been discountenanced. Until very recently, these mineral resources, from political motives, were little referred to; or it was imagined by all the governments that have preceded the present one, that by allowing their exploration, it would tend to prostrate and annul the agricultural spirit and industry of the people. We have no opinion to offer for or against the soundness of this idea; we only affirm that this is not the principle of the present administration of Hayti, which invites laborers of the African race to come over and participate in the exploration and the riches to be obtained from these mines, which henceforth are no longer closed.

* This chapter is contributed by Dr. Smith, of Port-au-Prince. It is not a translation.

Few countries are more highly favored in the variety and value of metallic ores, and none can boast of so general or natural distribution of them, as Hayti. On the present occasion, little more is required than a summary note of certain known localities in these parts of the country. In the North St. Michel, the parishes of Lemonade, Dondon, Plaisance, and Port de Paix, are mineral districts; the neighborhood of Jacmel; the Mirebalais, Lascahobas, and Banica, in the West and East Northeast, are among the most interesting mineral sections of the Republic. The South has also its portion of this species of natural wealth. Iron is everywhere profusely distributed under the form of the Peroxide,—hœmatite, the carburet, pyrites, or the sulphuret. Detached pieces of magnetic iron are often met with. The country abounding everywhere in wood, smelting establishments and founderies would quickly realize the hopes of the most sanguine and ambitious. Extensive mines of coal (Lignite) are about being utilized by the Government; those already known are located, one at a short distance from the town of Aux Cayes, at "Camp-Perin," and the other, in the Northeastern section of the Republic, in the vicinity of the Artibonite River. There are other natural depots of this invaluable mineral, situated in other parts, but the above ones, in extent, appear to be inexhaustible, and are still more valuable from the facility of transport offered by their location.

Gold quartz and copper, antimony and silver, the jasper and marble, talc, jet, and the agate, are among the providential dotations that are most abundantly and generally diffused in and about the mountain ranges of Hayti. Copper is seen under different forms and in different places. The most common are the blue and green pyrites, mixed often with the sulphuret of iron, at other times separate. The red, blue, and green oxyd, or malachite, under the blowpipe will yield from 35 to 45 per cent. of copper, but these are not the richest in Hayti. Salines are numerous. Rock, or gem salt, is a natural production. Sulphur and saltpetre are to be procured by a little manipulation and industry, and, in fact, to terminate, it may be said, without fear of contradiction, that Hayti, up to this time, has been known only as an agricultural State, and remains yet to be known in reference to its great and varied mineral advantages.

W. G. Smith.

VI.

Soil.

W. S. COURTNEY, Esq., in a recent volume on "The Gold Fields of St. Domingo," written with the object of inducing a white emigration to the Dominican Republic,—*a purpose which it is impossible to accomplish peacefully*,—describes accurately the nature of the soil of the Eastern part; and, as what he says of it applies equally to Hayti, I herewith transcribe and subjoin it: "The soil of the Island of St. Domingo is constituted of the *debris* of the mountains and hills and the decayed vegetation of past ages. When we reflect that these prodigious mountains differ remarkably and essentially in their geological constituents, and that the contrast is truly striking, sometimes between mountains and even hills in juxtaposition, it will appear how endless would be the task of speaking definitely and particularly of all the various kinds of soil that are to be found on the Island. The soil of the valleys, slopes, and plains, partaking of the characteristics of the hills and mountains on, beneath, beside, and betwixt which they are found, varies as they vary. In one place we find a rich vegetable mould; in another, a mixture of this mould with pebbles and sand; in another, a light, loose, spongy loam; in another, a loose marl; in another, a clayey marl; in another, a soil formed of dissolved or pulverized coral and shells; and in another, of pure clay or sand. It differs, also, in color and depth as much as it differs in constitution and quality. Sometimes it is yellow, though still retaining its productive qualities; sometimes it is red, sometimes of a bluish cast, sometimes of a dark, muddy, or lava color; but most generally it is black, and its depth varies from ten feet to six inches. In the valleys and slopes, in and on the mountains, and on the savannahs and plains, it is generally a rich, black loam, varying in depth from three to ten feet. In the lowlands, on some of the coasts, it is a salt meadow or quagmire, without any solid bottom, except where the roots of the mangrove ramify and interlace so as to retain the vegetable portion of it carried there by the streams, while further back it is formed into a solid earth, bearing abundance of marine-figs, flags, sea-rushes, and tall grass. The deepest and richest soil is found in the valleys, at and near the mouths of the principal rivers, and is made up of the alluvial deposits brought down by these streams. So variable are the nature and characteristics of the soil, that it often radically changes in passing from one side of a valley to another, or crossing a stream, and sometimes differs essentially on the opposite banks of the rivers; and often, in passing along the road, it will be observed to change in the course of a few rods, or even feet. In the larger valleys and plains, especially some distance from the mountains, it is more uniform; and more uniform on the South side of the Island than in the interior and on the North side. . . . . On some of the mountains and their elevated slopes the soil is good, and the grass and other similar undergrowth grow dense and rank to their very tops, while the elevated portions of others sustain only broken and ragged forests of pitch pine, interspersed with palm and many hard and durable woods. Others of these mountains are again bald and sterile on their tops and around their summits, peering up through the green and heavy foliage below like naked cones. An analysis of the soil, at different places, attests the fact that it is highly impregnated with the minerals peculiar to the mountains, which probably accounts for its variety in color in different localities. It has been found to contain iron, sulphur, copper, antimony, mercury, gold, cobalt, manganese, salt, and other minerals in various combinations and conditions at different points. The gold is of course found pure and diffused in the soil almost all over the Island, in some places being only very slightly traceable, and in others palpably so. In regard to the productiveness of the soil, suffice it to say that, notwithstanding its diversity and variety, it is prolific beyond anything found in the Antilles, and not excelled by that of the Italian peninsula or Sicily, to which it bears a strong resemblance. The sugar-cane grows the year round, and so fast and thick, that by the time the laborer has cut over and exhausted a ten-acre field, it is ready again to cut where he began. The corn, which is cultivated now by simply making a hole in the ground and dropping in the seed, with no further care or labor, grows to the height of from eight to fifteen feet, bearing three to five ears to the stalk. The tobacco, which is cultivated with as little scientific skill and care, spreads out the broadest and sappiest leaves found anywhere in the Antilles. Other crops indigenous to the climate grow with equal rapidity and strength. It is said that in some districts the melon, the pumpkin, and the squash ripen in six weeks from the seed. [At Port-au-Prince radishes ripen in three weeks from the time of planting the seed. J. R.] . . . Such a thing as a *fertilizer*, an article of such extended traffic and so necessary to the agriculturist here, is not known nor thought of there, nor will it, I apprehend, ever be required. The fertility and strength of the soil, containing all the elementary constituents required to produce and mature the various vegetable growths, could not be exhausted even without any return to it for generations. Besides, the mountains themselves are the great fertilizers of St. Domingo, and will remain so until they are devoured by the tooth of time and sink away in distant ages. The *debris* of these mountains, together with the decaying vegetation on their sides and tops, brought down by frequent rains, supply the soil in the valleys, plains, and savannahs, with abundant and incessant recruits. Its fecundity is a marvel to the husbandman of these latitudes

VII.

Climate, Seasons, and Temperature.

FROM the geographical position of Hayti, and its proximity to Cuba and Jamaica, a non-resident might infer that the climate and atmospheric range of temperature which prevail in either one of the Antilles were common to all, and strictly alike and similar in reference to this Island.

This is not exactly the case. Its peculiar situation in respect to the other Antilles and to the influence of the trade winds, and many other natural circumstances besides, operating propitiously, have given to Hayti much advantage in these respects over her sister isles of the same group. We affirm, from experience, that the climate of Hayti is more healthful, that the range of temperature is less ardent, than in the neighboring islands; that the reasons as to why this should be so appear too various, too multiplied, to admit our specifying any one in particular. The fact, however, cannot be contested; so that, whether from the altitude of its several chains of mountains, the one out-topping the other, and on the lofty heads of which the surcharged clouds are condensed or dissolved into rain; the extent and fertility of its plains and valleys, everywhere most liberally intersected by rivers, streams, mountain torrents settled into placid rills, which, under the solar influence, undergo constant evaporation, that refreshes and tempers the air; whether these combined, together with its topography, its physical configuration, and its ever-green, exuberant forests, which are everywhere spread out, and which reach up to the very tops of the mountains, the foliaceous undulations of which exercise perpetually a cooling influence on the surrounding torrid atmosphere; whether there be other causes or reasons beside these, we do not assert; but we think it rational to conclude that all these circumstances, operating incessantly, are the real agencies that modify and soften the climate of Hayti, and have rendered its temperature milder, less sultry, and more salubrious than it is found to be in Cuba or Jamaica during parallel seasons.

A country blessed with all these natural advantages must enjoy also great variety of climate and varied degrees of temperature, as regards a residence in the plains and a more or less proximity to the seaboard, or a graduated approach to the more elevated parts, upwards, towards the higher mountain range. Its capacity to produce every kind of vegetable substance that can contribute to the comfort of its inhabitants and to the prosperity of the state, must be equal to the fecundity and diversity of its soil.

Hayti, rich in all the variety of tropical productions, is well adapted, in its elevated situations, to the growth of most all those grains and plants that thrive in other latitudes and cooler regions. The peach, the apple, strawberries, the raspberry, the cauliflower, potatoes, the carrot, the beetrave, the broccoli, parsnip, and the asparagus, and other like legume and esculents, have all been long ago naturalized in this country, and they flourish as vigorously as in Europe or America.

Besides the multitude of floral families, species, and their varieties common to the tropics, the rose, the violet, the pink, *(l'œillet,)* geraniums, diversify and decorate our alpine valleys, which are likewise carpeted spontaneously with the clover and the daisy, while the oak, the common fir, and exalted pine-tree, *(pinus sylvestris,)* are multiplied into forests whose extent are estimated by the leagues of country they cover, and which are only within a few leagues' distance from several points on the seacoast.

Four seasons are distinctly sketched, but *three* only annually can be said to be well marked, persistent, and immutable in these parts, that is to say, the Western, the Northern, and the Southern Departments or sections of the Island, which all who immigrate are destined to inhabit. These comprehend two wet or rainy seasons and one dry season, which, in relation to each Department and particular localities, vary as to the time when they commence, but occur most always about the period of the equinoxes and solstices. In the Western Department, Port-au-Prince, the seat of government, is located. There, the rainy season is in February, March, and April. During these months more or less rain falls irregularly through the day. The latter part of May, June, and July, to about the middle of August, with certain rare exceptions, comprehends the *dry* season, and is the hottest part of the year. The rainy period returns towards the end of August, and continues through September to about the middle of October, and is then succeeded by what is called by the European resident, the cool, delicious season.

Thermometer, hottest season, from 10 A. M. to 4 P. M., in the shade, maximum, 98° Fahrenheit; same time, *in the sun*, 120° to 121°. Out of town, in the plains, several degrees lower. At *Grand-fond*, situated E. S. E., distant but three or four hours' ride from the capital, in July, the thermometer at 6 A. M. will mark 59° to 60°, and from 12 M. to 2 P. M., 72° to 78° maximum. From the end of October during the rest of the year, and up to the following month of April, the thermometrical range, in the shade, from 10 A. M. to 3 P. M., is 85° to 90° maximum; in the sun, 110° to 115° Fahrenheit.

The Northern Department, with Cape Haytian as its principal town, has *two* seasons, strictly speaking. December, January, March, and April, are rainy months. What is denominated the *dry* season commences in May and is prolonged through August and September. The highest range of temperature is in August, when the North wind is not dominant. Thermometer, in the shade, from 11 A. M. to 2 P. M., 85° to 92°. In the plains it is never so high as in the town at the same period of the year. On the more elevated parts, as in Lemonade, etc., for example, the thermometrical range is seldom over 72° to 85° maximum.

The Southern Department, principal town Aux-Cayes, is usually under the influence of rains during the months of May, June, and July. August and September mark the *dry* season in that section of the island. From November to March the air is cool and salubrious at Aux-Cayes, and still more so in the plains and rural districts, where the temperature is always several degrees less than it is in situations near the seacoast. The thermometrical range is referred to thát of Port-au-Prince and the West.

The reader of this imperfect exposition of the climate, seasons, and temperature of Hayti will be convinced at once of the causes of the extraordinary fertility of its soil, and will perceive the advantages which must result from industry and agricultural enterprise properly conducted in such a country.

W. G. SMITH, *of Port-au-Prince.*

COPPER COINS OF HAYTI.

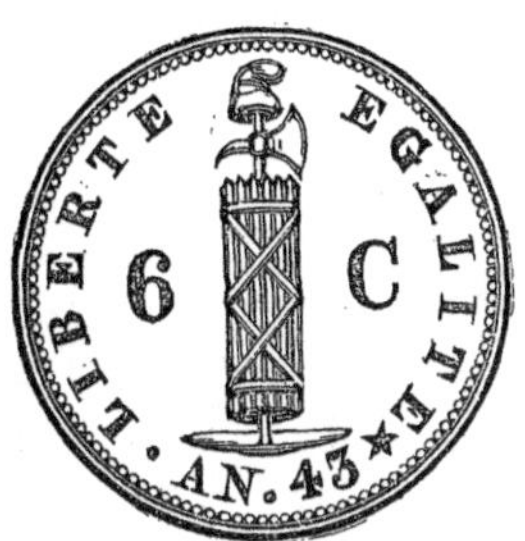

Book Second.

THE REPUBLIC AND EMIGRATION.

OFFICIAL PART.

I.

Editorial Introduction.

INSTRUCTED by the Government to publish in full all its laws and other documents in relation to emigration, I herewith subjoin them without abridgment; although, necessarily, there are occasional repetitions of facts and of guarantees in them, made in reply to similar questions, or in reviewing the action that has been taken with a view of carrying out the grand and generous project of the Chief of the Republic and his enlightened counsellors, — that of making Hayti to the black race what England is and has been to the proscribed and persecuted classes of Europe, a safe place of refuge, not only, but a free and a powerful fatherland.

I prefix a translation of the Constitution of 1846, which Soulouque abolished, but the Republic revived, with certain Modifications rendered necessary by the altered circumstances of the times. The Modifications, also, are appended. It will repay a careful study to the general reader; to the emigrant it will be invaluable for reference.

The documents are arranged in the order of their dates, and it will be observed that the terms become more liberal as these advance.

One word of explanation is rendered necessary in view of the editor's appointment as the General Agent of Emigration in America, and the passage of the Homestead Bill in Hayti. No emigrants will be entitled to a free passage, or have the right of drawing $15.00 from the treasury on their arrival in the Island, unless furnished with the certificate of the Bureau of Boston. Those, also, who accept a free farm, will be expected to pay their passages; but if unable, for the moment, to do so, the necessary means will be provided for them, and abundant time be allowed them, after their arrival in the Island, to refund the advance. In order to prevent an emigration to Hayti of persons who would leave this country for the country's good, it will also be demanded from applicants for a homestead, that, if from the Northern States or the Canadas, they shall produce the certificate of the Bureau of Boston. Of course, this rule will not be enforced in the case of emigrants from that barbarous and blood-stained section of the Union where black men are enslaved, and white men who sympathize with them so often suffer death at the hands of the mob,—even, as recently in Texas, the fearful torture of the stake.

It is not the design of the Bureau of Boston to send emigrants, except in peculiar cases, by transient vessels; but to charter ships expressly adapted for the purpose of conveying them comfortably and speedily. In these vessels, those who desire to pay their own expenses will be accommodated at the lowest rates, both as regards board and passage money; while the others will receive equal consideration and attention. All emigrants, unless special provision be made for large companies, will sail from the port of Boston.

II.

Constitution of Hayti.*

THE Haytian people proclaims, in presence of the Supreme Being, the present Constitution of the Republic of Hayti, in order to consecrate for ever its rights, its civil and political guarantees, its sovereignty, and its national independence.

TITLE I.

OF THE TERRITORY OF THE REPUBLIC OF HAYTI.

ARTICLE 1. The Island of Hayti and the adjacent Islands which are dependent thereon, form the territory of the Republic.

2. The Territory of the Republic is divided into departments. Their limits will be established by law.

3. Each department is subdivided into arrondissements, each arrondissement into communes. The number and boundaries of these subdivisions shall also be defined by law.

4. The Republic of Hayti is one and indivisible, essentially free, sovereign, and independent.

Its Territory is inviolable, and cannot be alienated by any treaty.

---

* Commonly called the Constitution of 1846, or the Constitution of Riché.

TITLE II.

OF THE HAYTIANS AND THEIR RIGHTS.

SECTION I.

Of the Haytians.

5. Are Haytians, all individuals born in Hayti and descended from Africans and Indians, and all those born in foreign countries of Haytian parents.

Are also Haytians, all those who, up to the present time, have been recognized as such.

6. All Africans or Indians and their descendants, are able to become Haytians.

The law settles the formalities of naturalization.

7. No white man, whatever be his nationality, shall be permitted to land on the Haytian territory, with the title of master or proprietor, nor shall he be able, in future, to acquire there either real estate or the rights of a Haytian.

SECTION II.

Of Civil and Political Rights.

8. No slave can be held on the Territory of the Republic; slavery is forever abolished.

9. All debts contracted through traffic in men, are annulled forever.

10. The right of asylum is sacred and inviolable in the Republic, except in the exceptional cases foreseen by law.

11. The union of civil with political rights constitutes the quality of citizen.

The exercise of civil rights is independent of the exercise of political.

12. The exercise of civil rights is regulated by law.

13. Every citizen, above the age of 21 years, exercises political rights, if he has, besides, the other necessary conditions determined by the Constitution.

Nevertheless, naturalized Haytians are not admitted to this exercise, till after one year's residence in the Republic.

14. The exercise of political rights is forfeited;

(1.) By naturalization in a foreign country;

(2.) By forsaking the country in a moment of imminent danger;

(3.) By accepting, without authorization, public functions or pensions conferred by a foreign government;

(4.) By serving, without authorization, either in the army or the navy of a foreign power;

(5.) By all settlement made in a foreign country without intention of returning.

Commercial establishments can never be considered as having been made without intention of returning.

(6.) By peremptory and final condemnation to perpetual punishment, at the same time both corporal and ignominious.

15. The exercise of political rights is suspended.

(1.) By the condition of hired servants;

(2.) By the condition of simple or fraudulent bankrupt;

(3.) By the condition of judicial interdict, of accusation, or of contumacy;

(4.) In consequence of a judicial sentence, carrying with it the suspension of civil rights;

(5.) In consequence of a judgment, decreed for a refusal to serve in the National Guard.

The suspension ceases with the causes which occasioned it.

16. The exercise of political rights can only be forfeited or suspended, in the cases mentioned in the preceding articles.

17. The law regulates the cases in which political rights may be recovered, also the means to be made use of and the conditions to be fulfilled to attain this object.

SECTION III.

Of Public Rights.

18. All Haytians are equal before the law.

They are all equally eligible to the civil and military services.

19. There exist in the State no distinction of orders, no distinction of birth, no hereditary powers.

20. Individual liberty is guaranteed. No one can be arrested or detained, except in the cases determined by law, and according to the manner by it established.

21. In order to the execution of an act, which decrees the arrest of any person, it must, 1st, set forth formally the motive of the arrest, and the law in execution of which it is decreed; 2d, emanate from a functionary to whom the law has formally given this power; 3d, be notified to the person arrested, and a copy left him.

All arrests that the law has not prescribed, or made without the required forms, all violence or rigor employed in the execution of a mandate, are arbitrary acts which every one has a right to resist.

22. No one can be forced to appear before any other judges than those that the Constitution or the law assigns him.

23. The house of every person, resident on Haytian Territory, is an inviolable asylum.

No domiciliary visit, no seizure of papers can take place, except by virtue of the law and in the forms prescribed.

24. No law can have a retroactive effect.

25. No punishment can be instituted except by law, nor imposed, except in the cases determined by law.

26. The Constitution guarantees the inviolability of property.

27. The Constitution also guarantees the alienation of the national domains, as also the grants of land made by the Government, either as a national gratuity or otherwise.

28. No one can be deprived of his property, except on account of public utility, in the cases and manner established by law, and in consideration of a just and previous indemnity.

29. The punishment of confiscation cannot be established.

30. Every citizen owes his services to the country for the

maintenance of liberty, equality, and property, whenever the laws summon him to defend them.

31. The punishment of death shall be confined to certain causes which the law shall determine.

32. Every man has the right of expressing his opinions on every subject; he may write, print, and publish his thoughts.

No control before publication can be exercised upon any writing whatever.

The abuse of this right is defined and repressed by law, without, however, affecting the liberty of the press.

33. All kinds of worship are equally free.

Every one has the right of professing his religion and of exercising freely his worship, provided he does not disturb the public order.

34. The establishment of a church or chapel, and the public exercise of worship, may be regulated by law.

35. The ministers of the Catholic, Apostolic, and Roman religion, professed by the majority of Haytians, will receive a stipend fixed by law. They shall be specially protected. Government determines the territorial extent of the parishes to which they minister.

36. Instruction is free, and schools will gradually be established to meet the wants of the people.

37. Trial by jury is established in all criminal matters. From its decision there is no appeal.

38. The Haytians have the right of association; this right cannot be submitted to any precautionary measure; the right belonging to the public authorities, of watching and prosecuting any association which may propose ends contrary to public order, is nevertheless maintained.

39. The right of petition is exercised personally, by one or several individuals, never in the name of a body.

Petitions can be addressed either to the executive or to either of the two legislative chambers.

40. The secrecy of letters is inviolable.

The law determines who are the agents responsible for the violation of the secrecy of letters confided to the post.

41. The use of languages used in Hayti, is optional; it can be regulated only by law, and only for the acts of public authority, and for judicial matters.

42. Public debts contracted either at home or abroad, are guaranteed. The Constitution places them under the safeguard and loyalty of the nation.

TITLE III.

OF SOVEREIGNTY AND THE EXERCISE OF THE POWERS DERIVED THEREFROM.

43. National sovereignty resides in the total number of the citizens.

44. The exercise of this sovereignty is delegated to three powers.

Those three powers are: the legislative, the executive, and the judicial.

45. Each power is independent of the other two in its attributes, which it exercises separately. None of them can delegate its authority or overstep the boundaries assigned to it. Each of the three powers is responsible for its own acts.

46. The legislative authority is exercised collectively by the chief of the executive and by two representative chambers, the chamber of deputies and the senate.

47. The executive authority is delegated to one citizen, who assumes the title of President of Hayti.

48. The judicial authority is exercised by a court of appeal, and other civil tribunals.

49. Each public functionary is personally responsible for his own acts.

A law will be passed to regulate the mode of proceeding against public functionaries for misconduct during their administration.

CHAPTER I.

OF THE LEGISLATIVE POWER.

SECTION I.

Of the Chamber of Representatives.

50. The chamber of deputies is composed of representatives from the arrondissements of the Republic.

The number of the representatives shall be fixed by law.

Each arrondissement shall have at least two representatives.

51. Until the law shall have fixed the number of representatives to be elected by the arrondissements, this number is settled as follows:

Five for the arrondissement of Port-au-Prince, *three* for each of the arrondissements which have chief towns of departments, and for those of Jacmel and Jérémie, and *two* for each of the other arrondissements of the Republic.

52. The representatives are elected as follows:

Every five years, from the 10th to 20th January, the primary assemblies of the communes meet, in conformity with the electoral law, and name each three electors.

53. From the 1st to 10th February, the electors of the communes of each arrondissement meet in the chief town, and form an electoral college.

The college names, by ballot, and by absolute majority of votes, the number of representatives to be supplied by the arrondissement.

It names as many substitutes as representatives.

54. These substitutes, by order of nomination, succeed the representatives of the arrondissement in case of death, resignation, forfeiture, or in the case provided by the article 60.

55. The half at least of the representatives and substitutes shall be chosen among the citizens who have their political domicile in the arrondissement.

56. To be elected representative or substitute, it is necessary to be —

(1.) Above the age of 25 years.

(2.) In the enjoyment of civil and political rights.

(3.) Possessed of real estate in Hayti.

57. The naturalized Haytian must, besides the conditions prescribed in the preceding article, prove a residence of three years in the Republic in order to obtain election as representative or substitute.

58. The functions of representative are incompatible with those of the administration of the finances.

A representative who exercises at the same time another function paid by the State, cannot draw two salaries during the session; he must choose between the two.

59. The judges, etc. of the civil courts, and the public officers attached to these courts, cannot be elected as representatives within the jurisdiction of the court to which they belong.

The members of the court of appeal, and the public officers attached to this tribunal, cannot be elected representatives within the jurisdiction of the civil court of Port-au-Prince.

The commanders of arrondissements and their assistants, the commanders of communes and their adjutants, cannot be elected representatives within the extent of their arrondissement.

60. Any representative who accepts, during his term of service, an office paid by the State, other than that occupied by him before his election, ceases thenceforth to be a member of the chamber.

61. The representatives are elected for five years.

The re-election is general.

They are indefinitely eligible to re-election.

62. During the whole time of the legislative session, every representative will receive from the public treasury a salary of two hundred gourdes a month.

He is besides allowed one gourde per league, for travelling expenses, from his commune to the seat of government.

SECTION II.

Of the Senate.

63. The Senate is composed of thirty-six members. They are elected for nine years.

64. The Senators are elected by the chamber of representatives on the proposition of the President of Hayti, as follows:

At the session which precedes the time of the renewal of the Senators, the President of Hayti makes a general list of three candidates for each Senator to be elected, which he forwards to the Chamber. Three candidates are taken from amongst the whole of the citizens.

65. The Chamber of Representatives elects, from the candidates proposed on the general list, a number of Senators equal to that of the Senators to be replaced.

This election is made by ballot, and by absolute majority of votes.

66. The Chamber of Representatives forwards to the Senate a report declaring the nomination of the Senators, and at the same time informs the President of Hayti of this nomination.

67. The Senate make known their nomination to the elected Senators, and invites them to appear and take the oath. This formality finished, the Senate reports it to the President of Hayti.

In case of death, resignation, forfeiture, etc., the Senate likewise informs the President of Hayti and the Chamber of Representatives of the vacancies to be filled up.

68. In no case can the sitting representatives be included in the lists addressed to the Chamber by the President of Hayti.

69. In order to be elected Senator, it is necessary to be —

(1.) Above 30 years of age.

(2.) In the enjoyment of civil and political rights.

(3.) Possessed of real estate in Hayti.

70. The naturalized Haytian must, besides the conditions pre-

scribed in the preceding article, prove a residence of four years in the Republic, in order to obtain election as Senator.

71. The functions of Senator are incompatible with all other public functions, except those of Secretary of State, and of Agents of the Republic abroad.

Nevertheless, a soldier may be appointed Senator; but if he accept the office, he ceases to exercise every military function, and must choose between the emolument of Senator and that of his rank.

72. Any Senator who accepts, during his term of service, the office of Secretary of State, ceases thenceforth to be a member of the Senate, unless, offered again as candidate by the executive, he be re-elected by the Chamber of Representatives.

73. Every Senator receives from the public treasury a salary of two hundred gourdes a month.

74. The sessions of the Senate are permanent. They may, however, be adjourned at any time except during the legislative session.

75. On the adjournment of the Senate, a permanent committee shall be left in its place. This committee shall be unable to pass any resolution except for the convocation of the Senate.

SECTION III.

Of the Exercise of Legislative Power.

76. The seat of the legislative power is the Capitol of the Republic.

Each Chamber has its own place of meeting.

77. The Chamber of Representatives meets every year on the first Monday in April.

The opening of its session may be made by the President of Hayti in person.

78. The legislative session lasts three months. In case of need, it can be prolonged to four, either by the legislative body or by the executive.

79. In the interval of the sessions, and in case of emergency,

the executive can convoke the Chambers to any extraordinary meeting.

It gives them a reason for this measure by a message.

It can also, as the case may require, convoke the Senate alone, during its adjournment.

80. The President of Hayti can also prorogue the legislative session, provided it takes place at another period, in the same year.

81. The Chamber of Representatives can be dissolved by the President of Hayti; but, in this case, he is bound to convoke a new one within a delay of three months at the utmost; and then the elections must take place according to the requirements of Articles 52 and 53.

82. The Legislative Chambers represent the entire nation.

83. The Chamber of Representatives verifies the commissions of its members and decides all controversies which may arise on the subject.

The Senate likewise examines and decides whether the election of the Senators has taken place in conformity to the Constitution.

84. The members of each Chamber take individually the oath to maintain the rights of the people, and to be faithful to the Constitution.

85. The sittings of the Chambers are public; nevertheless, each forms itself into a secret committee whenever it thinks proper.

The deliberation which arises in a secret committee is made public, if the Chamber so decides.

86. No one can be at the same time a member of both Chambers.

87. The Legislature makes laws on all objects of public interest.

The initiative belongs to each of the two Chambers and to the Executive. Nevertheless, every law relating to public receipts and expenses must first be voted by the Chamber of Representatives.

88. The authoritative interpretation of the laws is given in the ordinary form of laws.

89. Neither of the two Chambers can pass any resolution, unless an absolute majority of its members be assembled.

90. Every resolution is passed by the absolute majority of votes, except in cases defined by the Constitution.

91. The votes are taken by the Senators rising or remaining seated. In case of doubt, the roll is called, and the votes are then recorded by *Yes* or *No*.

92. Each Chamber has the right of inquiry into all things appertaining to it.

93. No project of law can be adopted by one of the Chambers, until each separate article of it has been passed.

94. Each Chamber has the right to amend and divide the articles and amendments proposed.

An amendment voted by one Chamber can be included in the articles of the law, only when it shall have been adopted by the other Chamber.

The organs of the Executive have the power to propose amendments to projects under discussion by virtue of the initiative possessed by the Chambers.

95. Every law passed by the two Chambers is immediately forwarded to the Executive, which has the right to object thereto.

When objections are made, the law is sent back to the Chamber in which it was first voted, and the objections notified. If they are approved, the law is amended by the two Chambers, and promulgated by the Executive.

96. If the Executive makes objections to a law adopted by the two Chambers, and if these objections are not approved by these Chambers, or by one of them, the Executive has a right to refuse its sanction to the *law*.

Nevertheless, if a dissolution of the Chamber of Representatives should happen thereon, and if the same law were again voted by the two Chambers, the Executive would be bound to promulgate it.

97. The approval of objections, and the amendments to which they may give rise, are passed by the absolute majority, in conformity with the Article 90.

98. The right of objection must be exercised within the following delay, namely: —

(1.) Within eight days, for laws of emergency, without the objection being in any case grounded on the emergency.

(2.) Within fifteen days for other laws.

But, if the session be closed before the expiration of this latter delay, the law remains adjourned.

99. If, within the delay prescribed by the preceding article, the Executive make no objection, the law must be immediately promulgated.

100. A project of law, rejected by one of the Chambers, or by the Executive, cannot be reproduced in the same session.

101. The laws and other acts of the legislative body are rendered official by means of a bulletin printed and numbered, entitled *bulletin of laws*.

102. The law dates from the day of its promulgation.

103. The Chambers correspond with the President of Hayti, in all matters concerning the administration of public affairs; but they cannot, in any case, call him to their bar, to account for any act of his administration.

104. The Chambers correspond likewise with the Secretaries of State, and with each other in the cases prescribed by the Constitution.

105. To the Senate alone appertains the right of naming the President of Hayti. This nomination is made by election by ballot, and by a majority of two thirds of the members present in the assembly.

106. In case the office of President of Hayti should become vacant, during the adjournment of the Senate, its permanent committee shall summon it to meet without delay.

107. The Senate has the right of approving or rejecting treaties of peace, alliance, neutrality, commerce, and other international conventions agreed to by the Executive.

Nevertheless, all treaties stipulating sums chargeable to the Republic, must be likewise submitted to the sanction of the Chamber of Representatives.

108. The Senate gives or refuses its approbation to projects of declaration of war submitted to it by the Executive.

It can, under serious circumstances, and upon the proposal of the Executive, authorize the momentary removal of the seat of government to another place than the capital.

109. No one can present petitions in person to the Chambers.

Each Chamber has the right to refer to the Secretaries of State the petitions addressed to it. The Secretaries of State may be invited to explain their contents, if the Chamber think fit, and if the Secretaries of State, being called upon, do not consider such publicity likely to compromise the interest of the State.

110. The members of the legislative body cannot be excluded from the Chamber to which they belong, or at any time called to account, accused, or tried, for opinions or votes pronounced by them in the exercise of their functions.

111. No member of the Chamber of Representatives can be arrested, during the session, or within the six weeks which shall precede or follow it.

Within the same delay, no member of the Chamber of Representatives can be prosecuted or arrested for matters criminal, correctional, or of police, (except in case of notorious criminal offence,) until the Chamber shall have permitted his prosecution.

112. No Senator is liable to apprehension during his continuance in office.

A Senator cannot be prosecuted or arrested for matters criminal, correctional, or of police, while in office, (except in case of notorious criminal offence,) until the authorization of the Senate be obtained.

113. If a member of the legislative body be apprehended, (in a case of notorious criminal offence,) the opinion of the Chamber to which he belongs is taken without delay.

114. In criminal cases, inducing punishment both corporal and ignominious, every member of the legislative body is placed under accusation by the Chamber to which he belongs.

115. The Senate forms itself into a high court of justice to decide on accusations made against members of the legislative body, against Secretaries of State, or any other great public functionaries.

The form of procedure before the high court of justice, will be determined by a law.

116. Each Chamber, by its by-laws, settles its own discipline, and defines the manner according to which it discharges its duties and exercises its privileges.

CHAPTER II.

OF THE EXECUTIVE.

SECTION I.

Of the President of Hayti.

117. The President of Hayti is elected for life.

118. In order to be elected President of Hayti, it is necessary —

(1.) To be born in Hayti.

(2.) To have attained the age of 35 years.

(3.) To be possessed of real estate in Hayti.

119. In case of vacancy through the death, resignation, or forfeiture of the President of Hayti, the Secretaries of State, assembled in council, exercise, on their own responsibility, the executive power.

If the President happen to be unable to exercise his functions, the Council of Secretaries of State is charged with the executive authority so long as the hindrance shall last.

120. Before entering on his duties, the President of Hayti takes before the Senate the following oath:

"I swear to the nation to discharge faithfully the duties of President of Hayti; to maintain with all my might the Constitution and the laws of the Haytian people; to enforce the respect due to the national independence and the integrity of the territory."

121. The President causes to be attached to the laws and other acts of the legislative body, the seal of the Republic, and sees that they be promulgated after the delays fixed by Articles 95, 96, 98, and 99.

122. The promulgation of the laws, and other acts of the legislative body, is in these terms:

"*In the name of the Republic,* —

"The President of Hayti directs that the above (law or act) of the legislative body be stamped with the seal of the Republic, published, and executed."

123. The President causes to be enacted the laws or other acts of the legislative body promulgated by him.

He makes all the regulations, decrees, and proclamations necessary to this effect.

124. The President names and dismisses the Secretaries of State.

He names and dismisses, also, the agents representing the Republic to foreign powers and governments.

125. He names all civil and military functionaries, and fixes their places of residence, if not already done so by law.

He dismisses removable functionaries.

126. The President of Hayti commands and directs the forces by land and sea, and confers rank in the army, according to the law.

127. He makes treaties of peace, alliance, neutrality, commerce, and other international conventions, with the sanction of

the Senate, and that of the Chamber of Representatives in the cases fixed by the Constitution.

He proposes to the Senate declarations of war when circumstances appear to demand it. If the Senate approve these projects, the President of Hayti declares war.

128. The President of Hayti provides, according to law, for the exterior and interior security of the State.

Every measure taken by the President is previously discussed in the council of Secretaries of State.

129. The President of Hayti has the right to pardon and to commute sentences. The exercise of this right shall be fixed by law.

He can also exercise the right of amnesty, but for political offences only.

130. No act of the President can have effect unless countersigned by one Secretary of State, who, by this alone, makes himself responsible.

131. At the opening of each session, the President, through the Secretaries of State, presents to the Senate and the Chamber of Representatives the general situation of the Republic, as well exterior as interior.

132. The President of Hayti receives from the public treasury an annual salary of forty thousand gourdes.

He resides at the national palace of the capital.

SECTION II.

Of the Secretaries of State.

133. There are four Secretaries of State, whose departments are fixed by the decree calling them to office.

The attributes of each department are determined by law.

134. The Secretaries of State compose a council under the presidency of the President of Hayti, or of one of their number delegated to that office by the President.

Every deliberation is recorded on a register, and signed by the members of the council.

135. They have right of entrance in both the Chambers to support projects of laws and objections from the Executive, or to make any other communication from Government.

136. The Chambers can require the presence of the Secretaries of State, and can summon them to answer for every act of their administration.

The Secretaries of State thus summoned, are bound to enter into explanations, unless they consider such a course liable to compromise the interest of the State.

137. The Secretaries of State are respectively responsible, as much for the acts of the President which they countersign, as for those of their department, as also for the non-execution of the laws.

In no case can the verbal or written order of the President, received by a Secretary of State, relieve this latter from responsibility.

138. The Chamber of Representatives has the right of accusing the Secretaries of State. If the accusation is admitted by two thirds of the votes, they are cited before the Senate, which then forms itself into a high court of justice.

139. Each Secretary of State enjoys an annual salary of five thousand gourdes.

Travelling expenses are allowed them by law.

SECTION III.

Of the Institutions of Arrondissements and Communes.

140. A council for each arrondissement, and a council for each commune, are hereby established.

These institutions are regulated by law.

CHAPTER III.

OF THE JUDICIAL POWER.

141. Litigations which have for their object some civil right are exclusively within the jurisdiction of the tribunals.

142. Litigations which have for their object political rights are within the jurisdiction of the tribunals, save the exceptions established by law.

143. No tribunal, nor other court for the settlement of disputes, can be established but by virtue of a law.

No extraordinary commission or tribunal can be created under any denomination whatsoever.

144. There is, for all the Republic, a Court of Appeal, the organization and attributes of which are determined by law.

The Court of Appeal has its sittings in the capital.

145. The law determines, likewise, the organization and attributes of the other tribunals.

146. The judges cannot be dismissed except for offence of bribery legally tried, nor suspended except on account of an approved accusation.

Nevertheless, the justices of the peace are liable to be dismissed.

147. Every judge may be called upon to urge his claims to superannuation, if he be in the conditions stipulated by law on the matter.

148. No one can be named judge or judicial officer unless he have attained the age of thirty years for the Court of Appeal, and of twenty-five years for the other tribunals.

149. The President of Hayti appoints and dismisses the judicial officers attached to the Court of Appeal and the other tribunals.

150. The functions of judge are incompatible with any other public function, except those of representative.

Incompatibility, by reason of relationship, is settled by law.

151. The salaries of the members of the judicial body are fixed by law.

152. Tribunals of commerce can be established. The law regulates their organization, their attributes, and the time of service for their members.

153. Special laws regulate the organization of the military

tribunals, their attributes, the rights and obligations of the members of these tribunals, and their length of service.

154. The sittings of the tribunals are public, unless such publicity endangers public order and good morals; in this case, the tribunal declare this by a decree.

155. The law regulates the mode of proceeding against the judges, in case of crimes or offences by them committed, either in the exercise of their functions or otherwise.

CHAPTER IV.

OF THE PRIMARY ASSEMBLIES OF COMMUNES, AND OF THE ELECTORAL COLLEGES OF ARRONDISSEMENTS.

156. Every citizen above the age of twenty-one years has the right of vote in the primary assemblies, if he be moreover a landed proprietor, if he have the cultivation of a farm, or if he practise a profession, fill a public office, or follow any business defined by the electoral laws.

157. To be a member of the electoral colleges, it is necessary to be twenty-five years of age, and be, besides, in one of the other positions mentioned in the preceding article.

158. The primary assemblies have the right of meeting, by virtue of Article 52 of the Constitution, or on the convocation of the President of Hayti, in the case mentioned in Article 81.

Their object is to appoint electors.

159. The electoral colleges meet likewise in their own right, by virtue of Article 53 of the Constitution, or on the convocation of the President of Hayti, in the case laid down in Article 81.

Their object is to name the representatives and their substitutes.

160. The meeting of two thirds of the electors of an arrondissement constitute an electoral college, and all elections are decided by the absolute majority of the votes of the members present and by ballot.

161. The primary assemblies and the electoral colleges can have no other object but the elections respectively assigned to them by the Constitution.

They are bound to dissolve when this is accomplished.

TITLE IV.

OF THE FINANCES.

162. No tax for the benefit of the State can be established, but by law.

Taxes for the use of communes and arrondissements are established by special laws.

163. No privileges can be granted in the matter of taxes.

No exception or abatement of taxes can be established, except by a law.

164. Except in cases formally excepted by law, no contribution can be levied from the citizens, unless as a tax for the use of the State, of the arrondissement, or of the commune.

165. No pension, no gratuity, chargeable to the public treasury, can be granted, except in accordance with a law.

166. The budget of each Secretary of State is divided into chapters. No sum allowed for one chapter can be carried to the credit of another, and employed for other expenses, without a law.

167. Every year, the Chambers decree, 1st. The account of receipts and expenses during the year or preceding years, for each department separate; 2d. The general budget of the State containing details of the receipts, and the funds assigned for the year to each Secretary of State.

Nevertheless, no motion, no amendment, can be introduced into the budget, to the end of reducing or augmenting the salaries of the public functionaries, and the pay of the soldiers, already paid by special laws.

168. The Chamber of Accounts is composed of a certain number of members fixed by law.

They are named by the President of Hayti, and hold office at his will. The organization and attributes of the Chamber of Accounts, are fixed by law.

169. The law settles the standard, the weight, the value, the stamp, the effigy, and the denomination of the currencies.

TITLE V.

OF THE PUBLIC FORCES.

170. The public force is raised to defend the State against exterior enemies, and to insure at home the maintenance of order and the execution of the laws.

171. The army is essentially obedient,—no armed body can deliberate.

172. The army is placed on peace or war footing, as occasion requires.

No one can receive soldier's pay unless he serve in the army.

173. The mode of recruiting for the army is fixed by law.

It regulates, likewise, the promotion, the rights and obligations of the soldiers.

174. No privileged corps can ever be created; but the President of Hayti has a special guard, subject to the same military rules as the other corps of the army.

175. The national guard is organized by law.

It can be mobilized, entirely or in part, only in the case mentioned in the law or its organization.

176. Soldiers cannot be deprived of their rank, honors, and pensions, but in the manner fixed by law.

TITLE VI.

GENERAL MEASURES.

177. The national colors are blue and red, placed horizontally.

The arms of the Republic are the Palm-tree, crowned with the cap of Liberty, and ornamented with a trophy of arms, with the motto, *l'union fait la force*, (union is strength.)

178. The town of Port-au-Prince is the capital of the Republic and the seat of government.

179. No oath can be administered except by virtue of the law. The form thereof is fixed by law.

180. Every foreigner who happens to be on the territory of the Republic, enjoys the protection given to persons and goods, save the exceptions established by law.

181. The law establishes a uniform system of weights and measures.

182. The national holidays are, that of the Independence, the 1st January; that of Alexander Pétion, the 2d April; that of Agriculture, the 1st May; that of Philip Guerrier, the 30th June.

The legal festivals are fixed by law.

183. No law, no decree, or regulation of public administration is binding, until published in the form prescribed by law.

184. No place, no part of the Territory, can be declared in a state of siege, except in case of civil troubles, or of invasion impending, or effected, on the part of a foreign force.

This declaration is to be made by the President of Hayti, and must be countersigned by all the Secretaries of State.

185. The Constitution cannot be suspended, either in whole or in part.

TITLE VII.

OF THE REVISION OF THE CONSTITUTION.

186. If experience demonstrate the inconvenience of some of the measures of the Constitution, the proposal of a revision of these measures can be made in the usual form of the laws.

187. If the Executive and the two Chambers agree upon the changes proposed in one session, the discussion of them shall be deferred to the session of the following year. And if, in this second session, the two Chambers again agree with the Executive upon the proposed changes, the new decrees adopted

shall be published in the usual form of the laws, as articles of the Constitution.

188. No motion of revision can be carried out, no change in the Constitution can be adopted by the two Chambers, unless on a majority of two thirds of the votes.

TITLE VIII.

TRANSITORY MEASURES.

189. The existing members of the Senate are maintained in office, as follows: —

One third for three years; one third for six years; one third for nine years.

This decree shall be executed by the Senate, by the drawing of lots at a public sitting.

190. In future, every Senator shall be elected by the Chamber of Representatives, for nine years, in accordance with Article 63 of the Constitution.

191. The formation of the Chamber of Representatives shall take place, for the first time only, as follows: —

The President of Hayti shall forward to the Senate a general list of three candidates for each Representative, and each substitute to be elected for each arrondissement.

The Senate shall elect, from among the candidates named in the general list, the numbers of Representatives and substitutes fixed by Articles 51 and 53 of the Constitution.

192. In the session of 1847, there shall be proposed to the legislature: —

(1.) A law regulating the mode of proceeding against public functionaries, for misdeeds committed by them during their administration.

(2.) A law regulating the form of proceeding before the high court of justice.

(3.) A law regulating the exercise of the right of pardon and of commutation of sentences.

(4.) A law regulating the retirement of judges.

(5.) A law fixing the attributes of the Secretaries of State.

193. The present Constitution shall be published and executed throughout all the extent of the Republic.

The codes of laws, civil, commercial, penal, and of criminal prosecution, together with all other laws thereto relating, are maintained in force until they be legally repealed.

All measures of laws, decrees, resolutions, regulations, and other acts, which are contrary to the present Constitution, are hereby annulled.

Given at the National House of Port-au-Prince, the 14th day of November, 1846, in the 43d year of the Independence of Hayti.

LAW MODIFYING THE CONSTITUTION OF THE FOURTEENTH OF NOVEMBER, 1846.

The legislative body, availing itself of the "initiative" conferred by Article 87 of the Constitution,

Seeing the decree of the Committee of Gonaïves, dated the 23d December, 1858, which revives, with modifications, the Constitution of 1846,

Considering the importance of making these modifications without delay, has passed unanimously the following laws: —

ARTICLE 1. The Articles 62, 71, 73, 111, 132, 133, 139, 167, and 182, are modified in the following manner:

ART. 62. During the legislative session, each Representative receives from the public treasury, a monthly salary, the amount of which will be fixed by law.

Another law shall likewise fix the amount to be allowed to each Representative for travelling expenses, from his commune to the seat of government.

ART. 71. The duties of Senator cannot be discharged by any one who may have other public duties devolving upon him.

Nevertheless, a soldier may be elected Senator, but thenceforth he ceases to exercise any military duty.

Art. 73. Each Senator receives from the public treasury a salary, the amount of which is fixed by law.

Art. 111. No Representative of the people can be imprisoned during the time that he holds his commission.

Nevertheless, if a Representative discharge any public duty after the session, he can be prosecuted for acts of which he may be guilty, and that before the ordinary tribunals.

Art. 132. The President of Hayti receives from the public treasury a salary, the amount of which is fixed by law.

He resides at the National Palace at the capital.

Art. 133. There will be from four to seven Secretaries of State, as the President of Hayti may judge necessary. Their departments will be fixed by the decree containing their nomination.

The duties of each department are determined by law.

Art. 139. Each Secretary of State will receive an annual salary, the amount of which will be fixed by law.

The amount of travelling expenses to be allowed to the Secretaries of State shall likewise be determined.

Art. 167. Each year the Chambers pass: 1. The account of receipts and expenses, accompanied by vouchers of the preceding year for each department separately; 2. The general budget of the State, containing the statement of income, and the moneys proposed to be allotted for the year to each Secretary of State, for the business of his department.

Nevertheless, no proposal, no amendment can be introduced into the budget to the end of reducing, or augmenting the salaries of the public functionaries, and the pay of the soldiers, already fixed by law.

Art. 182. The National holidays are: that of the *Independence of Hayti*, the 1st January; that of *T. T. Dessalines*, the 2d January; that of *Alexander Pétion*, the 2d April; that of *Agriculture*, the 1st May; that of *Philip Guerrier*, the

30th June; that of the *Restoration of the Republic*, the 22d December.

ART. 2. The Articles 189, 190, and 191, of the same Constitution, are suppressed; the Article 192, which by this decision becomes 189, is modified as follows:—

ART. 189. In the session of 1860, if not before, there shall be proposed to the legislative body:

(1.) A law regulating the mode of proceeding against public functionaries for acts of their administration.

(2.) A law regulating the form of procedure before the high court of justice.

(3.) A law regulating the exercise of the right of pardon and the commutation of sentences.

(4.) A law regulating the retirement of the judges.

ART. 3. The Article 193, which now takes the No. 190, shall be drawn up as follows:

ART. 190. The present law shall be published and executed throughout the whole extent of the Republic.

The codes of civil, commercial, and penal laws, those of criminal prosecution, and all laws relating thereto, are maintained in force until legally repealed.

All the provisions of laws, decrees, resolutions, regulations, and other acts which are contrary to the present Constitution are hereby annulled.

Given at the National House, at Port-au-Prince, the 14th day of July, 1859, in the 50th year of the Independence.

The President of the Senate..... HILAIRE JEAN–PIERRE.
The Secretaries .... S. TOUSSAINT, B. INGINAC.

Given at the Chamber of Representatives, at Port-au-Prince, he 15th of July, 1859, year 56th of Independence.

The President of the Chamber.. PANAYOTY.
The Secretaries.............. J. THÉBAUD, B. GUILLAUME.

In the Name of the Republic,

The President of Hayti ordains that the law subjoined, of the Legislative Corps, be sealed with the seal of the Republic, published, and executed.

Given at the National Palace of Port-au-Prince the 18th of July, 1856, year 56th of Independence.

Geffrard.

By the President:

The Secretary of State, President of the Council........ J. Paul.
The Secretary of State, of Justice, and of Worships, charged with the portfolio of the Interior, and of Agriculture.. F. E. Dubois.
The Secretary of State, of War, and of the Marine.... T. Déjoie.
The Secretary of State of the General Police.......... Jh. Lamothe.
The Secretary of State of Finances, and of Commerce.. Vn. Plésance.

III.

Letter to the Editor.

LETTER TO THE PRESIDENT.

PORT-AU-PRINCE, AUG. 4, 1859.

TO HIS EXCELLENCY THE PRESIDENT OF HAYTI:

In behalf of certain blacks, and persons of color in the United States and the Canadas, who are desirous of emigrating to Hayti, I respectfully ask replies to the following questions:

I. Would Emigrants be subject to military duty? If so, for how long, and what manner of duty?

II. Would you grant such Emigrants perfect liberty to leave the country whenever they desired to do so?

III. Would they be required, directly or indirectly, to support the Roman Catholic Religion if they are not members of the Catholic Church?

IV. How long ere they would be invested with all the rights, civil and political, of native-born Haytians?

V. Do you guarantee to such Emigrants as efficient governmental protection as is given to the native Haytians?

VI. Is the Government willing that such Emigrants should settle in neighborhoods? Is the Government prepared to sell such tracts, on easy terms, to be paid in instalments, or within a reasonable number of years, and what other facilities and encouragements will the Government give to introduce such an emigration, and such settlements of communities? I ask your particular attention to this head, as, unless it is satisfactorily answered, it will be impossible to induce an emigration of wealthy and intelligent men from America.

VII. Provided such settlements were formed, what educational facilities would be extended them?

I have the honor to be, &c.,

JAMES REDPATH.

REPLY OF THE GOVERNMENT.

Office of the Secretary of State of Foreign Relations,
Port-au-Prince, August 17, 1859.

Sir: I have the privilege of transmitting to you the replies to the questions contained in your letter of the 4th instant, to His Excellency the President of Hayti, relative to emigration.

It is chiefly to the development of Agriculture in Hayti, that the Government wishes to make this enterprise subservient.

To that end it is disposed to accord special favors to persons of that profession who shall decide to emigrate. To agriculturists, and to those who shall come here with the intention of devoting themselves to cultivation, it will accord the following advantages:

First, It will pay their passage at the rate of fifteen piastres (Spanish or American dollars) for each able-bodied man or woman; and at that of eight piastres for children of twelve and under, and old persons beyond sixty years.

Second, It will board and lodge them for eight days, while they are seeking other accommodations.

It may be proper to explain here the usage respecting contracts which are ordinarily formed between agriculturists and proprietors in the country. The proprietors advance the lands and works, (usines,) the agriculturists undertake the cultivation and improvements; the produce is equally divided between the proprietor and agriculturist. The emigrants may each make contracts if they see fit. The emigrants will find land to buy from private individuals. They may also obtain it from the Government, and at a reasonable price, on easy terms of payment, if the State possesses land in the districts where the emigrants shall establish themselves.

The Government will extend to them the same protection as to Haytians themselves. For the rest, shortly after their arrival in the country, they can have the same civil and political rights as the Haytians; for, according to the civil code of Hayti, every person descended from African or Indian blood, can, certain formalities fulfilled, become a Haytian after a residence of one year in the country. The religious belief of the emigrants, to whatever Christian sect they may belong, shall always be respected. They shall freely exercise their worship. There shall never be occasion to call them to defend the Roman Catholic religion, whether they believe it or not.

A recent law fixes the term of obligatory military service for every Haytian at nine years. The citizens required for this service are designated by lot. The Government, as an evidence of its good intentions in favor of emigration, has resolved to exempt the emigrants from military service. But this exemption shall not extend to their children when they shall have attained the prescribed age of drawing lots.

The emigrants shall make a part of the National Guard, (militia.) The National Guard meets only on the first Sunday of each month, and has no exercises to make on that day. In case of extraordinary events, a more active service may be exacted of it. But then it will be a duty to fulfil for the guaranty of the general interests, and consequently of their own.

The emigrants will be permitted to settle together, in each locality, as much as it shall be a practicable thing; but they shall not, therefore, cease to be subject to the laws and authorities of the Republic.

The present Government, which is devoting itself seriously to spreading light, has founded, and will continue to found, numerous primary schools. In these institutions instruction is given cheaply, and even gratuitously, to certain children.

The children of the emigrants shall enjoy in this respect the same advantages as those of Haytians.

Our laws deprive no one of the privilege of leaving the country if they please; nevertheless, the Haytian who abandons his country in the moment of imminent danger loses forever the quality of citizen. The emigrants who do not wish to remain in Hayti are free to re-embark; yet those whose introduction into the country shall be at Government expense, can leave only after a residence of three years.

This, sir, is the communication that I have been charged to make to you. Accept the assurance of my distinguished consideration.

The Secretary of State of Foreign Relations:

A. JEAN SIMON.

IV.

Call for Emigration.

MEN of our race dispersed in the United States! Your fate, your social position, instead of ameliorating, daily becomes worse. The chains of those who are slaves are riveted; and prejudice, more implacable, perhaps, than servitude, pursues and crushes down the free. Everything is contested with us in that country in which, nevertheless, they boast of liberty; they have invented a new slavery for the free, who believed that they had now no masters; it is this humiliating patronage which is revolting to your hearts. Philanthropy, in spite of its noble efforts, seems more powerless than ever to lead your cause to victory. Contempt and hatred increase against you, and the people of the United States desire to eject you from its bosom.

Come, then, to us! the doors of Hayti are open to you. By a happy coincidence, which Providence seems to have brought about in your behalf, Hayti has risen from the long debasement in which a tyrannical government had held her; liberty is restored there. Come and join us; come and bring to us a contingent of power, of light, of labor; come, and together with us, advance our own common country in prosperity. We will come by this means to the aid of the philanthropists who make such generous efforts to break the chains of those of our brethren who are still in slavery.

Our institutions are liberal. The government is mild and

moderate. Our soil is virgin and rich, — we have large tracts of good land, nearly all uncultivated, which only need intelligent workmen to till them. Everything assures you in this country of a happy future. For those among you who possess capital, it will be easy to find at once a place among us. The country offers them immediate resources. They can count on the solicitude of the Government, and on its special protection. Our society is ready to adopt them, and prepares for them a fraternal welcome. They will enjoy here all the considerations that they merit; they will occupy the rank that their respectability assigns them,— all the things that a blind and barbarous prejudice refuses to them in countries inhospitable to our race.

The poorer emigrants shall have the right to all that their situation demands. The Government will provide for their first necessities, and will take the proper measures to secure to them a quiet and honorable asylum, as well as to facilitate for them the means of obtaining employment.

It is very natural that you should ask, before coming to an unknown country, what are the facilities that will be afforded to you, as well for the satisfaction of your first needs, as for your definitive settlement. This thought has seriously occupied the Chief of the Republic and his Government.

I proceed to state the determination to which it has come:—

To such of you as are not able to pay the expenses of your passage, aid will be given from the public treasury.

Agents, whom I shall presently appoint in the United States, will be charged to make the necessary arrangements in this respect.

On their arrival here, the emigrants will find lodging gratuitously, where, during the first few days, their needs will be provided for.

Government will occupy itself from this time with providing means to offer to each person, on arrival, either on private estates or the public domains, sufficiently remunerative work.

Every individual, the issue of African blood, may, immediately on arrival, declare his wish to be naturalized: and after one year's residence, he can become a citizen of Hayti, enjoying all his civil and political rights. *

The emigrants will be exempt from military service, but their children, when they are of the requisite age, shall be held to perform the service conformably to the laws of the country; that is to say, for a limited time, and by the result of conscription. [*Par suite du tirage au sort.*] This exception does not constitute, in their favor, a modification of the law on the National Guard, of which every citizen must form a part.

You will have power, also, freely to exercise your religion.

I have spoken here only of the members of the African race, who groan in the United States more than elsewhere, by reason of the ignoble prejudice of color; but our sympathies are equally extended to all those of our origin who, throughout the world, are bowed down under the weight of the same sufferings. Let them come to us! The bosom of the country is open to them also. I repeat it, they will be able to acquire, either on the public or private estates, fertile lands, where, by the aid of assiduous labor, they will find that happiness which, in their actual condition, they cannot hope to find.

The man whom God has pointed out with his finger to elevate the dignity of his race, is found.

The hour of the reunion of all the children of Hayti is sounded! Let them be well convinced that Hayti is the bulwark of their liberty!

Given at the office of the Secretary of State of the Interior, at Port-au-Prince, the 22d August, 1859, Fifty-Sixth year of Independence.

The Secretary of State, of Justice, and of Worship, charged *par interim*, with the portfolio of the Interior and of Agriculture.

F. E. DUBOIS.

V.

Answers to Questions Presented by Mr. Newman.

PORT-AU-PRINCE, MARCH 26, 1860.

WE are desirous to receive amongst us all men of African origin who are willing to share our fortunes.

The reception given at St. Marc, to one hundred and twenty emigrants from Louisiana, is a proof of the good-will of the country people as regards these persons.

When they arrive here they will find, either to lease or buy, from the Government or private parties, fertile lands at a reasonable price. For persons unacquainted with the country, and who have to study its peculiarities, the system of leases is not to be despised, the very small annual charge being no obstacle to the prosperity of their labors. Besides, the government is authorized by law to sell all national lands. They possess a great extent of land, in different parts of the country, and will always place their lands at the disposition of the emigrants. The mode of sale imposed upon them by law, in this case, is, *for cash.* In certain quarters these properties are sufficiently extensive to allow of the settlement of one hundred families or more.

Permission will be granted to emigrants to buy land, on their making the declaration that they wish to become Haytians, and on their renouncing every other nationality.

Our law authorizes the formation of two sorts of companies: Copartnerships, which do not need any preliminary authorization, and Joint Stock Companies, whose statutes would have to be submitted to the Government for their approval. It determines the conditions on which they exist, and their mode of action. Under the control of this legislation companies could be formed, either for exploring the mines, or for the establishment of manufactories, and the Government would look very favorably on all serious undertakings of this sort.

The Government cannot bind itself to the adoption of a protective tariff. Manufacturers would, however, have a sufficient guarantee in our actual tariff, whose mean rate for the last twenty years has been 20 per cent. upon the value of goods imported. As our fiscal legislation derives its principal revenue from the customs duties, it is not to be supposed that the existing system will be given up, for a long time to come.

We have no law on Patents. The principle, however, exists in our civil law, as regards literary property, and might, if need be, be developed, so as to afford protection to inventions.

Though the law of the National Guard prescribes a monthly review thereof, on every first Sabbath in the month, measures would be taken not to disturb the conscientious scruples of the members of those churches which forbid such a use of that day.

The sons of emigrants destined to a religious career will be exempted from military service. There will be no exception made in the case of those who may be engaged in secular pursuits or professions.

Provisions of all kinds being always to be had in abundance, there is no need of dispensing with the payment of the customs duties on provisions for the use of those who may arrive.

Machines, agricultural implements, and personal effects, will be allowed to be brought into the country free of duty. There can be no exception made to the general rule in such cases, as regards the disposal of produce by the emigrant.

The Government will engage to provide remunerating labor for honest and able, but poor laborers, who could not immediately purchase property. This they would do, either by means of leases or partnerships, or by placing them in such situations as, by economy and good conduct, they could in a few years become proprietors.

Lands for schools and chapels would be given by the State.

The emigrants would not be compelled to come to Port-au-Prince, but could go directly to that part of the country which they would choose.

They would, after the settlement of a year and a day in the Republic, enjoy all the privileges of Haytian citizens.

To make it easy for those needy persons of African origin who would wish to emigrate to Hayti, the Government has decided, since last year, to pay their passage, at the following rates: —

Fifteen dollars Spanish for every able-bodied man and woman. Eight dollars for children under twelve years of age, and for aged persons above sixty.

It is well to make known the contracts which are usually made in this country between agricultural laborers and proprietors. The proprietors give the land and necessary implements, the others cultivate the land and dispose of the produce. This is divided equally between the proprietor and the cultivator. The emigrants might enter into such agreements if they saw fit to do so.

The Government will always respect the religious belief of the emigrants, no matter to what Christian sect they may belong. They will never be called upon to defend the Roman Catholic religion, whether they follow it or not.

The present Government, in its earnest desire to spread knowledge among the people, has founded and will yet found a number of primary schools. In these establishments instruction is given cheap, and even gratuitously to certain children. The children of emigrants will enjoy in this respect the same privileges as Haytian children.

Our laws do not take away from any one the power to leave

the country when he pleases. Nevertheless, the Haytian who abandons his country in times of imminent danger, loses forever the right of citizenship. Those emigrants who do not care to remain in Hayti will be free to go back again. Those, however, whose passage the Government may have paid, will not be able to leave the country until after three years' residence.

These, sir, are the communications which I am commissioned to make to you.

The Secretary of State of the Interior and of Agriculture,

(Signed) Fs. Jn. Joseph.

VI.

Vacant Lands.

Office of the Secretary of State of the Interior and of Agriculture, Section of the Interior.

REPORT.

TO His Excellency the President of Hayti:

President:—I believe the time has come to submit to your Excellency the result of the labors undertaken by your order on the question of Emigration into our country of men of our race. After having examined, from different points of view, this important subject, it is time to substitute action for preliminary studies, and the more so that definitive questions are now proposed to the Government of the Republic. Men who have appreciated the riches of our soil, the mildness of our national manners, the working of our institutions, the good intentions of your Excellency, desire to put their hands to the work. Direct propositions have been addressed to us; demands for information have been made of us; time presses; they ought to be replied to.

On the other hand, we ought to state that in all that portion of our hemisphere which extends from the rivers St. Lawrence to Orinoco, a work of expulsion of populations is in progress, to which we ought not to remain inattentive. To profit by this movement in welcoming men of our blood, the victims of these outrageous persecutions, is to continue the work of rehabilitation undertaken by the Founders of the Republic, and to remain faithful to the National Traditions.

I will, firstly, place under your eyes what has been done by my predecessors and by myself to advance this question to a practical result; and then I will submit to your Excellency the conclusions which it seems to me proper to adopt.

On the 22d of August, 1859, the Government, by a circular of the Secretary of State of the Interior and of Agriculture, made an appeal to all persons of our race who suffer from the prejudice of color. Hayti offers them a refuge, and facilities to come and establish themselves among us. To agriculturalists, particularly, they guarantee an immediate position, in harmony with their pecuniary standing. They may become landed proprietors, farmers, or laborers on halves, [à moitié fruits,] or by the week. Those among them who had not the means of paying their passage would be received at the expense of the Government.

It was stated that the emigrants would be excused from military service, — the service of the National Guard alone being obligatory on all citizens.

Convinced of the importance of informing families who desired to come to our country, of the liberality of our Institutions in matters of religious belief, the Government guaranteed, conformably with the disposition of our laws, the public exercise of the worship that each of them professed.

This appeal was received abroad with numerous commendations, emanating as well from those who were themselves interested, as from the friends of humanity. It was a proof of the honorable position of the country which enabled us to throw afar off a ray of civilization.

But this first step made by our Government was only a general enunciation of generous intentions. Subsequent relations with men well disposed towards our race have called our attention to points of detail which it was useful to examine, or to which it becomes necessary to give precise replies.

The Government declared, first of all, that an absolute submission to the laws of the country was the principal condition. Liberal and republican, these laws offer [serious] guarantees to all. They satisfy, as well in regard to civil as to political order, all the legitimate wants of an advanced society. By making known their dispositions, an answer was given to many of the questions proposed. Meanwhile all the points of detail were not examined, though light was thrown upon them. Our interior state is little known abroad; we judged it necessary to dissipate all doubts which might exist in the minds of foreigners.

Thus, the Government said that it possessed, in all parts of the country, demesne lands in large tracts; that, among them, there were many of excellent quality; and that the laws authorized us to sell them;

That the price of them was moderate;

That, at different points, the extent was such that groups of a hundred to two hundred families would be able to establish themselves thereon;

That to each of these groups freehold sites would be granted for the establishment of schools and chapels, whatever might be the religious belief of the members of the settlements.

That, on their declaration of their intention to become Haytians, and renounce every other nationality, the emigrants would have the right of purchasing lands;

That, to honest laborers, vigorous but poor, who might not be in a position to purchase, it would give all desirable facilities for obtaining remunerative work, — either as farmers, as interested on shares, [that is, paying one half the crop as rent for the farm, houses, and manufactories,] or as day-laborers. By the profits arising from such work they would be enabled, in a short time, if they were men of economy, and well-behaved, to become prosperous;

That, further, the public treasury would pay the passage of this class of persons, at the rate of fifteen piastres (American dollars) for each adult man and woman, and of eight piastres for each child of less than twelve years of age, or aged persons over sixty;

That all the immunities which other citizens of the Republic enjoy, will be accorded to them, after a residence of one year in the Republic;

That the exercise of all religions was protected by our laws, and that our national manners guaranteed an unlimited tolerance to all beliefs;

That the formation of commercial companies, existing in other countries, was authorized by our laws;

That these laws recognize:—

Copartnerships,—which do not need any preliminary authorization;

Joint Stock Companies,—whose statutes would have to be submitted to the Government for their approval;

That, under the authority of this legislation, companies might be formed, as well for the exploitation of mines or forests as the establishment of manufactures;

That we have no patent-right laws, but that the principle exists in our civil law, and is capable of expansion;

That the Government cannot engage itself to encourage, by a protective tariff, articles which might be manufactured in Hayti; but that manufacturers will find a sufficient guarantee in our actual tariff, which has always averaged 20 per cent. on the cost price. As our fiscal legislation derives its chief revenues from Custom-House duties, it is not likely that it will, for some time to come, abandon the system;

That, the chief articles of food being always abundant, there is no necessity for emigrants bringing provisions from abroad, nor consequently of waiving the payment of the Custom-House duties thereon; but that machines, agricultural implements, personal baggage, and furniture, shall be free of entry;

That, as to the exportation of products, no change will be made in the present Custom-House duties;

That the cordial reception given at St. Mark to the Louisiana emigrants by our people, so naturally hospitable, was a proof of the cordial reception in reserve for those who may subsequently arrive;

That nothing shall contravene the religious scruples of those who regard it as a duty to abstain from all occupation on the Sabbath. It is proper to state, however, that the monthly review of the National Guard is held on the first Sunday of the month; but it will be easy to make a legal modification of this arrangement;

That a temporary lodging, for the first eight days, shall be offered to those arriving, until they get settled according to their wishes;

That, independently of the schools that these new citizens may create, the existing Government, which occupies itself without ceasing with the duty of public instruction, has founded, and will still found, numerous educational establishments in which the monthly charge is next to nothing, and gratuitous to the poor;

That our laws deprive no one of the right of quitting the country when he sees fit; yet, that the Haytian who deserts his country in the time of need, loses forever his quality of citizen. The emigrants who may not desire to remain in Hayti, will be at liberty to re-embark; but those whose introduction into the country shall have been at public cost, shall not be permitted to leave until after three years' residence, or until they repay to Government the expenses to which it has been put on their account.

The Government would not have its task regarded as complete if it had not collected the most circumstantial facts on every point relating to this grave question. After receiving the order from your Excellency, I addressed, on the 20th of March last, a circular to the commanders of the arrondissements and the councils of the communes, instructing them to lay before the population of the country the condition of men of African race abroad, and to ask from them an energetic co-operation, in the event that a great number of persons should resolve to take up their abode in Hayti. These circulars have been made public, and the responses they have called forth testify the most lively sentiments of fraternity. Extending to the administrators of finances in their capacity of managers of the national domains, this correspondence, which has been carried on rapidly, and of which it is only possible, President, to submit to you a synopsis, we have received proofs of a general good-will. Here there are offers of public subscriptions; there they wish to charge themselves with the care of a certain number of persons; in an infinity of places they will give [rent] lands on halves; some will rent, others sell them; in fine, all are disposed to make all proper arrangements.

The lists furnished by the administrators of finances are not complete. Though I had recommended them to omit small parcels of land, I am sure that I have many additions to receive; some have, moreover, been announced already.

Laying aside all information which does not seem sufficiently precise, I have caused a list to be made, arrondissement by arrondissement, following the rule of not going further from the sea than twelve to fifteen miles, so as not to lose the advantages of sea carriage. I have, nevertheless, made exceptions in favor of Mirebalais, Lascahobas, and Plaisance, to which localities there are tolerably good roads from Port-au-Prince and Cape Haytian.

Here follows the synopsis of this work.

ARRONDISSEMENT OF PORT-AU-PRINCE.

In different parts of the communes of the Croix des Bouquets and l'Arcahaie, there are vast lands, belonging to the State, and which offer the means of locating a good number of individuals. Independently of these lands, there are a great many individuals who possess extensive tracts which they would wish to see cultivated, either on lease or on half shares. According to general use, the machinery, etc., for the manufactory of sugar and syrup, on these properties, would be placed in the hands of those who would cultivate them. The great fertility of the plains of Cul-de-Sac, Boucassin, and l'Arcahaie, offers numberless advantages to emigrants; but if it were a question of purchasing, lands in these quarters are considerably dearer than in less central localities; this, moreover, is ever the case in the neighborhood of large towns. It is certain, nevertheless, that if serious offers were made for such properties, prices would fall considerably. This same observation which I here make can be applied to every part of the country.

Apart from the farmers of these properties, a thousand persons could probably find occupation there as laborers, sugar-boilers, machinists, and in other trades useful to agriculture.

ARRONDISSEMENT OF LÉOGANE.

This arrondissement has very few State lands which are not occupied, especially in the plain. From Gressier to Petit Goâve, a pretty large number of individuals could find employment.

But when we speak of private property, we here find, as in deed throughout all the Republic, a vast extent of land which is of no present use to the owners. Many of them are disposed, some to sell, some to lease, or to make any other arrangements which might prove reciprocally beneficial to the contracting parties. This important arrondissement possesses, within easy reach of the capital, beautiful rich plains, running down to the sea, and having a great many good landing-places. The navigation of the gulf of Port-au-Prince, easy at all seasons of the year, offers great advantages for the disposal of produce. The mountains produce superior coffee in great abundance, and their cool and fertile lands admit of the cultivation of all sorts of produce.

ARRONDISSEMENT OF ST. MARK.

From Mont Rouis to St. Mark, the State possesses, in the plains, considerable quantities of irrigated lands, of good quality, and several estates in the mountains. Several private parties in this quarter are willing to sell at moderate rates.

In the plain of the Artibonite, over an extent of sixty miles, from Verrettes to la Rivière Salée, there are a good many unoccupied State lands. These lands are fit for all sorts of cultivation, particularly of cotton, corn, and provisions. Towards Rivière Salée the deposits from the Artibonite have covered the lands with mud. They are easily cultivated, and can be used also for raising stock. There are ponds there which only require to be kept in order to furnish good water during the whole year. Private parties would also sell cheap large quantities of land.

In order to bring back to this arrondissement its ancient prosperity, the water-courses would have to be opened as formerly, and the channels which are now filled up would require cleaning.

The commander of this arrondissement makes this observation, that the principal inconvenience which he has met with here is the want of houses. You can go a long distance without meeting a single cabin, and experience has shown him that this is a serious obstacle for men who, on arriving, are obliged to spend considerable time to build themselves a shelter. I do not hesitate, President, to point out to you the arrondissement of St. Mark as one of the most important points for emigration. Here are vast tracts of land thinly peopled, and of known fertility, large rivers, easy communication, an open port, a town at an easy distance from two great commercial centres, easy communication with the arrondissements of Mirebalais, Lascahobas, and Marmelade; there are in this locality all the elements necessary to bring back its ancient riches. The only thing which is wanting is a population in proportion to its magnificent position. Emigration can supply this. We have already seen a certain number of Louisianians take this direction, and others are announced.

ARRONDISSEMENT OF MIREBALAIS.

The Government owns, in this arrondissement, a great amount of land. The mildness of the climate, and the fertility of the soil, offer very great advantages. Several proprietors offer large properties for sale.

This district would seem to be very favorable to men of our race who, from a long residence in the cold countries of North America, would find it difficult to accustom themselves to the much greater heat of the lowlands. The distance from any seaport would certainly be an inconvenience for the embarkation of produce, but the high road to Port-au-Prince, by way of the plain of Cul-de-Sac, is generally pretty good.

ARRONDISSEMENT OF LASCAHOBAS.

All that I have said of Mirebalais applies to this arrondissement. There is here a large quantity of land, both public and private property.

The land here is of prodigious fertility, and fit for all kinds of culture. Lascahobas has also vast deposits of coal, and if the Artibonite could be made navigable, this part of the country could attain to a high degree of prosperity.

ARRONDISSEMENT OF DESSALINES.

At a short distance from the village of Dessalines, the State owns from two thousand to twenty-five hundred acres of land, or more. Near to St. Mark, and placed in much the same circumstances, what has been said of the one applies to the other. As it is situated more in the interior, it may be considered as a continuation of the arrondissement of St. Mark. There are several questions which would require profound study, — such as the regulation of the water supply, the cultivation of different savannahs, etc.

ARRONDISSEMENT OF GONAÏVES.

This arrondissement must be joined to the two preceding ones, to complete a group, the unity of which is scarcely broken by the administrative divisions. In the centre, and forming a vast quadrilateral, is a magnificent basin (or hollow) watered by the Artibonite, the Ester, and various small water-courses. Cotton has always been grown on these lands, which are in a superior degree adapted to its cultivation. By giving them water, every kind of produce natural to this climate could be grown there.

The high road from St. Mark to Gonaïves intersects them, and there are numerous landing-places on the seashore.

ARRONDISSEMENT OF PORT DE PAIX.

There are many demesne lands in this section, of upwards of three hundred and six hundred acres each lot. The quantity of land situated in the plains is small compared to that on the hills and in the mountains. Both are very fertile, and would produce almost anything. Cotton would succeed well on the long line of country which extends from the Bay-des-Moustiques to the Bombardo.

The department of the northwest is only thinly peopled. Many private parties wish to come to terms of any kind with emigrants. Large lots of land could be found on very favorable terms. Twelve thousand acres are at present in the market.

Landing-places are numerous all along the coasts. Port de Paix, an open port, would facilitate the disposal of all sorts of produce. Besides, its nearness to Cape Haytian presents important advantages.

I do not speak of the arrondissement of Mole St. Nicholas, as this part of the country is very poor and barren.

ARRONDISSEMENT OF THE BORGNE.

As in almost every place, the Government lands are more abundant in the mountains than in the plains, in this section. Private parties are open to arrangements with emigrants.

The climate is mild, and the lands are fertile. There is here a great variety in the cultivation of the land. Cocoa is the staple of several districts. There is a bright future awaiting this part of the country, in the matter of agriculture. The price of land is rather high. By means of many harbors and

10*

landing-places, this section has easy access to Port de Paix and Cape Haytian.

ARRONDISSEMENT OF LIMBÉ.

In all the department of the north there are great numbers of demesne lands in the hands of squatters, or of farmers who do not pay their rent. The conditions of their leases ought to be fulfilled by them. This they should be made to do under penalty of cancelling their leases.

This is an inconvenience which we often meet with in this district.

There is much waste land here, the climate is mild, and the lands very fertile. The sympathies of the emigrant will be attracted by its smiling and picturesque aspect, as those of the traveller invariably are.

Plaisance (the very name indicates the advantages to be enjoyed here) rejoices in a climate of imcomparable mildness, and of very great fertility. Though at a considerable distance from any commercial centre, it is, by its position, the principal market between the Cape and Gonaïves, and has the means of taking its produce to the most favorable of these two markets.

ARRONDISSEMENT OF CAPE HAYTIAN.

The Government lands are more parcelled out here than in many other localities; this is always the case in the neighborhood of large towns. There is, notwithstanding, a considerable quantity of demesne land. Six miles from the Cape, at Morne Rouge, there are seven hundred and fifty acres of unoccupied land. This virgin soil, of great fertility, is watered by numerous springs. Independently of being near the capital of the district, they are near the landing-place of Acul du Nord.

The fertility of the plain of the Cape is proverbial.

The sections of Limonade and Quartier-Morin, are justly renowned for their fertility. In spite of the heat of our climate, the cultivation of the sugarcane succeeds admirably without irrigation.

Many private parties, owning vast properties, are without workmen. This is a guarantee that emigrants will be able to come to terms with them.

ARRONDISSEMENT OF THE GRANDE RIVIÈRE.

The local authorities manifest much sympathy in behalf of emigration. Though the Government lands are cut up into small parts, or partly leased, there is room here for a good number of laborers. Many of the leases are only held for the cutting of the logwood. This fine arrondissement has a large extent of fallow land of first-rate quality.

ARRONDISSEMENT OF THE TROU.

Here there are numerous demesne lands. If the quality of the soil is not always equal to that of the arrondissements of which I have already spoken, there are, nevertheless, great advantages to be met with. The drier lands are specially adapted to the growing of cotton.

ARRONDISSEMENT OF FORT LIBERTÉ.

This is one of the districts which offer the largest extent of Government land. Tracts of vast extent, in the plains as well as in the mountains, could be placed at the disposal of the emigrants. There are good and numerous landing-places. Its nearness to Cape Haytian would largely facilitate the sale of produce of all sorts. It would be easy to establish, in this section, settlements and villages. The mountains which tower above this part of the island are rich in various minerals.

ARRONDISSEMENT OF NIPPES.

I now pass to the department of the South.

There is much sympathy shown, in the arrondissement of Nippes, on the question of emigration. The inhabitants are industrious, and on that account there are not so many large Government properties as elsewhere, but large quantities of land have been spontaneously offered for sale, on lease, or to be worked on half-shares. They would also pay the passage of one hundred laborers.

Near the seashore, the Government has but little land. At

Baradères, however, there are several unoccupied properties forming a lot, near the shore, of about twenty-four hundred acres.

The soil is very fertile, and fit for any kind of lowland cultivation. The river of Baradères flows along this land. Quite near this river, and joining the mainland, from which it is separated by a channel of little depth, is the Het à Pornic, measuring some twelve hundred acres of good land. These two lots would be a good site for a settlement of a thousand persons.

From twelve to eighteen miles from Miragoäne, is the Rochelois, a section of the country, of a mild climate, and of great fertility. Here there is about the same extent of vacant lands, belonging to individuals who are willing to come to terms.

This arrondissement has an open port, Miragoäne. It is within easy reach of Port-au-Prince and Jérémie, and offers real advantages for the disposal of produce, as well as for the purchase of the necessaries of life. There are numerous landing-places all along the shore.

ARRONDISSEMENT OF THE GRAND 'ANSE.

Jérémie, capital of this district, has the advantage (equally with St. Mark and Port de Paix) of possessing the most agreeable and salubrious climate in the whole Island. The soil in the neighborhood of Jérémie is fertile, and, being well watered, produces abundantly sugarcane, coffee, tobacco, cotton, cocoa, and all kinds of West India provisions.

In the plains, Government has no very great quantity of land, but private parties are in want of laborers to cultivate the vast extent of property belonging to them. They are disposed to make arrangements of different kinds. The harbor of Jérémie is open to foreign commerce, and flags of all nations wave there. Numerous landing-places facilitate the transport of produce.

ARRONDISSEMENT OF TIBURON.

In this, one of the most interesting districts in the country, Government owns a large extent of land. The ports of

Tiburon, Anse d'Hainault, Dame Marie, and Petite Rivière, are quite near to each other, and allow of easy communication. The inhabitants earnestly desire to see this plan of emigration succeed, and are ready to pay the passage of needy farm laborers, and would find them work, either by the day, on half shares, or on lease. The natural products are the same as at Jérémie. Cocoa is very largely cultivated, and there is room for great extension in this respect.

ARRONDISSEMENT OF CAYES.

In the commune of Cayes there is but little Government land, but from Torbeck to the Coteaux, and from this latter place to the Anglais and Port à Piment, (on the line from Coteaux to the Anglais,) there are many Government properties in lands of a fertile character. The population is tolerably scattered, and there are large vacancies to be filled up.

The plains of the South are justly celebrated for their great productiveness in the article of sugarcane. The inhabitants are industrious, and laborers would receive from them a hearty welcome. There is easy communication by means of numerous ports and harbors.

The port of Cayes offers an important market for all sorts of produce.

ARRONDISSEMENT OF AQUIN.

There are in this district large quantities of Government lands. It would be easy to find in the plains, in large parcels, at least 3,600 acres in the different communes. Besides this, private parties offer about the same quantity in large plantations, on very reasonable terms. They would also welcome a certain number of laborers. This district is very well disposed to second the views of the Government.

ARRONDISSEMENT OF JACMEL.

Coffee and provisions are the staples of this district; but near Saletrou and Marigot the land would grow cotton. The mountains grow all sorts of produce. The mountainous character of this district offers but little advantage to those who, on arrival, look for good roads and easy communication. If this plan of emigration should succeed to any great extent, no doubt its turn would come.

I have not mentioned in this report certain rich tracts of land in the interior, as in the arrondissement of Marmelade. I have not done so because I conclude that, at least for the time being, the absence of good roads is a sufficient obstacle to emigration. These splendid table-lands in the interior will, doubtless, one day have their turn. The fertile plains of Hinche, St. Michel, Banica, and Vallière, must necessarily attract attention. Their great metallurgic wealth, their coal deposits, and the mildness of their climate will recommend them as districts rich in promise for the future. The surveys which your Excellency will cause to be made will bring out in bold relief all these peculiar advantages.

I have taken no notice of mountain lands. It is nevertheless necessary to note here, that Government has many excellent lands of this kind. There is a needless alarm as to the difficulty of transporting produce in a hilly country. This should not be lost sight of, however, that in such parts of the country, much less labor is required; and that, besides provisions and vegetables, which grow there in abundance, coffee, cocoa, and cotton succeed admirably. It is easy to cultivate these things, and they do not require any large outlay. This should not be lost sight of. In all the districts of the Republic there are immense tracts of this description, — all they need is laborers.

These laborers are presenting themselves, President. If the small emigration from Louisiana seems to prefer the district of St. Mark, other proposals are made to us in view of the Northwestern section. All we have to do is to direct these currents to the points where the probability of success is greatest. The direction of agents abroad is necessary in order that our plan may succeed. It is quite natural for a man, before going to a foreign country, to wish to know what kind of resources it possesses.

The Government, on its part, should know as much as possible of the antecedents of intending emigrants.

Other measures will no doubt be subsequently needed, but they will perhaps require the intervention of the legislature.

The reasons which have given rise to the creation of emigration offices demand that these offices should be organized, at least, in those localities towards which emigration will most probably be directed in the beginning.

For the above-mentioned reasons, I have the honor to propose that your Excellency direct the following steps to be taken: —

1. That agents be appointed in foreign countries to promote an emigration into this country of men of our race.

2. That the towns of Cape Haytian, St. Mark, Port-au-Prince, Gonaïves, and Cayes, be named immediately as points where the emigrants can disembark. This measure to be extended, if necessary, to Port de Paix, Miragoäne, Jérémie, Aquin, and Jacmel.

3. That emigration offices be opened at Cape Haytian, Gonaïves, St. Mark, Port-au-Prince, and Cayes.

4. That two inspectors be named, in the North and South, to survey and make a plan of the Government lands.

5. That a certain number of small frame-houses, which could be easily put up, be sent for from the States, to be sold to such emigrants as may need them.

6. That each emigration office should have placed at its disposal a building where emigrants may be lodged on arrival, and that authority be given to provide for their wants during the first eight days after arrival.

7. Lastly, that 3,000 copies of this report be printed and sent to our agents in foreign countries.

(Signed) F. Jn. Joseph.

Port-au-Prince, August 6, 1860.

DECREE.

Fabre Geffrard, President of Hayti,

On the Report of the Secretary of State for the Interior and Agriculture;

Considering the Decree on Emigration of April 23, ultimo;

By advice of the Council of Secretaries of State,

Decrees as follows:

Art. 1. Agents will be appointed in foreign parts to promote emigration, and to give all needful information to intending emigrants.

Art. 2. An emigration office will be opened at St. Mark.

Art. 3. A building will be placed at the disposal of each emigration office, in which emigrants on disembarking will be received.

Art. 4. The towns of Cape Haytian, St. Mark, Port-au-Prince, Gonaïves, and Cayes, are named as points of disembarkation. This measure can be extended, if need be, to Port de Paix, Miragoâne, Jérémie, Aquin, and Jacmel.

Art. 5. Two inspectors will be named, for the North and South, whose duty it will be to survey and describe exactly such demesne lands as are disposable, with a view of settling emigrants upon them.

Art. 6. Wooden houses will be prepared beforehand, by the care of the Secretary of State for the Interior and Agriculture.

Art. 7. The present Decree will be printed, published, and put into execution by the Secretary of State for the Interior and Agriculture.

Given at the National Palace, Port-au-Prince, the 14th of August, 1860, the 57th year of Independence.

(Signed) Geffrard.

By the President:

The Secretary of State for the Interior and Agriculture,

(Signed) F. Jn. Joseph.

VII.

Laws in favor of Emigration.

FROM an official record of the proceedings of the Legislative Chambers of Hayti, we translate the following important documents.

SENATE. *Session of September*, 1860.

. . . . The President (of the Senate) announced to the organs of the Government that the Assembly was ready to receive their communications. The Secretary of State of the Interior rose and stated that his colleagues and himself were charged by the Government to submit to the Senate a project of law on emigration. He then made the following exposition of the reasons for the project:

Gentlemen: For many years past, tendencies to emigration, more or less decided, have appeared amongst men of our race on the American Continent and in the Islands of our Archipelago. Already, under the fallen government, an agent was sent to New Orleans to endeavor to profit by these dispositions, and the present administration, finding this work already begun, has sought to give to the movement a more vigorous impulse.

Recent facts were used as the starting-point to our efforts. A large number of the States of the great North American empire, in consequence of events which it is useless here to retrace, adopted a new policy, the rigors of which were destined to produce throughout the world a dismal echo. Our hearts were moved by the sufferings of our brethren on the other side of the water, and we conceived that a great duty was imposed upon our country. To the full extent which our laws allowed, we expressed, under different forms, our wishes and sentiments to the children of the African race. We have received proofs of their sympathy, and we know that in spite of offers and numerous efforts made to induce them to settle elsewhere, it is still towards Hayti that they turn their eyes.

But, gentlemen, we must not shut our eyes to the fact that, whatever advantage, whatever satisfaction emigration may secure, in the case of a family leaving their country for a distant one, there is always a certain fear of swallowing up their limited capital, and of remaining without resources in the face of an unknown future. Amongst the persons who wish to come, there is a large majority who, from their pecuniary position, are unable to run risks or trust to chance. Being possessed but of small means, they fear, on their arrival amongst us, being obliged to use their money in the purchase of an estate which they would be unable, from want of capital, to turn to good advantage.

Gentlemen, these considerations are important. Government has seriously reflected on the subject. It has, on the one side, consulted the duties of our exceptional nationality, and has asked whether, in the position which we occupy in the world, we are not called upon to fulfil great obligations towards our brethren, whose misfortunes are one of the calamities of the age. On the other side, in presence of our financial embarrassment, it has sought the best practical means to be made use of in order to destroy the material obstacle which separates us from men whose hearts yearn towards Hayti.

Thus put, the question, matured by more than a year's study, was destined to arrive at a solution worthy of the great men who have founded a country for the children of the African race. It is this solution, gentlemen, that I have the honor to submit to you.

Government proposes to grant five *carreaux* of land to every family of agriculturists, or laborers of African or Indian race. The grant shall be reduced to two *carreaux* for every unmarried cultivator or laborer.

This measure is the object of the first article of the law which I now submit to your deliberations. Articles 2, 3, and 4, are intended to regulate this decree.

You know, gentlemen, that at least two thirds of our lands are fallow lands. The State, although owning immense domains, derives scarcely anything from this enormous capital. And how can it be otherwise, when the labor necessary to cultivation is wanting, in consequence of our deficient population? Besides,—why not admit it?—we still practise the agricultural processes of the ancient colonists, while around us everything has progressed, agriculture and manufactures. The progress attained during the last quarter of a century has changed the mode of agriculture, as well as all other arts of production. To remain stationary, when others are making giant strides, would be exceeding dangerous for us.

In consequence of the recent decrees, by which we are enabled to recommence the sale of Government lands, we have sold and are still selling a few estates; but this operation produces no perceptible change in the general condition of national labor. It is scarce anything else but a removal of laborers. The measure we propose to you will, on the contrary, add to the number of our products, and tend to bring into general use the processes which give wealth to countries possessing a soil and climate identical with our own.

It is, then, with entire confidence that I lodge in your hands this project of law, destined to increase the prosperity and power of our beloved country.

After which, this high functionary read the said project of law and delivered it to the Bureau, which gave him a receipt in the name of the whole Senate.

Law on the Emigration into the Country, of Persons of African and Indian Race.

FABRE GEFFRARD, *President of Hayti,*

By the advice of the Council of the Secretaries of State,

Has proposed the following law:

ARTICLE 1. After the promulgation of the present law, five carreaux of land will be granted, free of all charge, to every family of laborers or cultivators of African or Indian race who shall arrive in the Republic. This grant will be reduced to two carreaux, when the laborer or cultivator is unmarried.

ART. 2. These grants will be delivered, without expense and with a provisional title, to every family that shall have made, before the proper magistrate, the declarations prescribed by law to the end of obtaining naturalization, and they will be converted into final grants after a residence of a year and a day in the country.

ART. 3. The final grants will be given in exchange for the provisional grants, only when it shall have been ascertained by the Government agent that cultivation has already commenced on the property granted.

ART. 4. The grantee shall not have the power to dispose of his grant before the expiration of seven consecutive years of occupation. Nevertheless, he will be able to obtain the authority to exchange his grant for another property, but only on the conditions, terms, and with the provisos above named.

The present law shall be promptly executed by the Secretary of State of the Interior and of Agriculture.

National Palace of Port-au-Prince, the 1*st September,* 1860, *year fifty-seventh of Independence.*

GEFFRARD.

BY THE PRESIDENT:

The Secretary of State, of the Interior, and of Agriculture. FS. JN. JOSEPH.
The Secretary of State, of War, and of Marine...... T. DÉJOIE.
The Secretary of State, of Justice, and of Worship.... E. DUBOIS.
The Secretary of State, of Finances, of Commerce, and of Exterior Relations............................ V. PLÉSANCE.
The Secretary of State of the General Police.......... T. LAMOTHE.

The Secretary of State of Justice and of Worship, took the floor [prend la parole] and presented the following project of law, which project, he said, the Government has considered as a measure corollary to the one just submitted to you, inasmuch as it is destined to realize and facilitate its execution, with regard to the formalities required to become a Haytian citizen, and to enjoy immediately the benefits of emigration.

Fabre Geffrard, President of Hayti,

On the report of the Secretary of State of Justice, and by the advice of the Council of Secretaries of State,

Considering that prompt action is demanded in behalf of those who possess the required qualifications to become Haytians, in order to enable them with facility to enter into the immediate enjoyment of the rights attached to naturalization,

Proposes the following law:

Article 1. Article 14 of the civil code is modified as follows:

"All those, who by virtue of the Constitution, are able to "acquire the rights of Haytian citizens, must, during the first "month of their arrival in the country, before the Justice of "the Peace of their residence, and in presence of two well-"known citizens, make a declaration to the effect that they "come with the intention of settling in the Republic. They "will, at the same time, before the Justice of the Peace, take "oath that they renounce every other country save Hayti."

Art. 2. Provided with the duplicate of the verbal process of the Justice of the Peace, setting forth their declaration that they come to settle in the Republic, and their taking of the oath, they will present themselves at the offices of the President of Hayti, to receive an act from the Chief of the State, recognizing them as citizens of the Republic.

Art. 3. The present law annuls all laws or measures which are contrary to it, and shall be executed with dispatch by the Secretary of State for Justice.

Given at the National Palace of Port-au-Prince, the 27th day of August, 1860, in the 57th year of Independence.

GEFFRARD.

BY THE PRESIDENT:

The Secretary of State for Justice, Public Worship, and Public Instruction,

DUBOIS.

The project was then remitted to the office, and a receipt therefor delivered to the Secretaries of State.

The Senate then read the first project of law. Its emergency was voted, on the proposal of Senator Jh. Essaleynes, supported by Senators Inginac and Zamor, Senior.

In consequence of this, the project underwent alternatively all the formalities required by the rules for the discussion of laws. The result thereof was that it was unanimously adopted in its principle, in its details, and as a whole.

On the adoption of the emergency proposed by Senator Labonté, with regard to the second project of laws, this project was also unanimously voted, in its principles, its articles, and as a whole. These acts were then drawn up in the official form, and were sent to the Chamber of Representatives, in conformity with the Constitution, where they were unanimously passed, without alteration or amendment.

Book Third.

ROUGH NOTES AND ESSAYS.

POLITICAL, SOCIAL, COMMERCIAL.

I.

The People of Hayti.

AS in all the Republics of the tropics and Central and South America, the people of Hayti are divided into two distinct parties, — the enlightened class and the uneducated mass. In Hayti we can discover, side by side with the highest intelligence and culture, many traces of the primitive superstitions and ideas. It is sufficient for the purpose of a Guide Book to speak briefly of both classes. The enlightened class may be described in three words: They are Frenchmen. All the distinguishing traits of the Parisian gentleman are reproduced in the educated Haytian. The uneducated class, and particularly the people of the country — *les habitans* — have the characteristics that are attributed to the inland Irish; they are hospitable, superstitious, of a never-failing good-nature, thoughtless of the morrow, with a quaint and prompt mother-wit, polite and sociable, but without ambition, and with little disposition to regular work. Their vices are contentment, petty theft, and a tendency to polygamy.

With these exceptions, they are characterized by all who know them, even by pro-slavery travellers, as essentially a good people, and capable of creating a great future. The aim of the fallen Government was to crush out the enlightened class, by encouraging the ancestral practices and ideas of the uneducated party; while all the energy of the present Administration is, by educational and other civilizing agencies, to exterminate ignorance with all its pestilential progeny. In this noble work, it is hoped, the emigrant will come in aid.

ORIGIN.

The blacks of Hayti are the descendants of between thirty and forty African races. These races, however, are now with difficulty recognized; and perhaps not half of them have pure representatives. They have mingled bloods, and become one people. In the days of slavery, the Congos were the most numerous of the imported blacks. Their chief characteristics were described to be, a genial disposition, a love of song and of the dance, an intelligent spirit, and a great fondness for plantains. The Senegals, the next in numbers, most nearly resembled the whites in character and feature; they had fine faces, and were distinguished by their silent habits, intellectual superiority, and bellicose disposition. The Yolofs possessed similar traits. The other imported races were the Calvaires, (from Cape Vert,) the Foulahs, the Bambaras, the Oniambas, the Mandingas, the Bissagots, the Socos. the Bourignis, the Cangas, the various tribes of the Gold Coast, the Ardras, the Caplavus, the Mines, the Agonas, the Sofos, the Fantins, the Cotocalis, the Popos, the Foëdas, the Fonds, the Aonssas, the Ibos, the Nagos, the Benins, the Mokos, the Mousombés, the Mondongas, and a few from Monomotapa, Madagascar, and Mozambique. The relics of their languages preserved in the Creole dialect, are largely of Congo origin; with the exception of some Vaudoux verses in which the Ardra and Canga tongues predominate. This circumstance, however, is owing to the facts that the Vaudoux worship is of Ardra origin, and that the Ardra tongue remained the language of its ceremonies.

There are very few traces of the Indian races in Hayti. The aboriginal inhabitants were utterly extinguished by the merciless and mercenary Spaniards. Of the imported Indians, one occasionally sees memorials in the longer hair and more regular beard than ordinarily belongs to the man of pure African descent. The present President had ancestors of partly Indian blood. Indians in Hayti have all the rights of Blacks.

LANGUAGE.

The language of the educated class, of commerce, of the Courts, and of the Court, is the French; and a knowledge of it is absolutely essential to every one who intends to reside in Hayti. Hence the emigrant should provide himself with the necessary text-books, and a Dictionary for the purpose of acquiring it. The language of the common people is *Creole.* From an essay on this dialect, written during my second visit to Hayti, I subjoin as much as is necessary for the guidance of the emigrant.

Haytian Creole, it is said, is easily acquired, but is so unlike the French that Frenchmen at first do not understand it. It presents three difficult elements to them: African words, French words mispronounced or abbreviated, and a peculiar grammatical or ungrammatical construction. There are several grades of this Haytian patois; some of them so nearly French that no translation is needed,—others so barbarous or bastard, (*le gros Creole,*) that hardly any resemblance can be traced to the mother tongue. The Creole of the Eastern Part, the missionaries say, is much more nearly like the Spanish, than the dialects of the West resemble the French tongue. In the lowest Creole, the proportion of African words is probably about one twentieth; but in the purest dialect the proportion is exceedingly small. "But the great speciality of the Creole," says Mr. Bishop, in a manuscript now before me, "is abbreviation. Conjunctions and pronouns are mercilessly sacrificed. This gives rapidity to the language. There is a low idiom used by the vulgar in distinction from that used by the more refined class. There is also a slight difference in different localities, similar to the provincial dialects in England, but not so widely different. The Creole can scarcely be acquired by any but a resident, and he must be a good hand at retaining words to do anything in it. A knowledge of it is essential to any one who has dealings with the lower class in the country, and small towns especially." Substantive plurals are unknown. They say *cheval* when they mean horses, and *cheval* when they speak of a horse. Accents are also changed. Instead of papièr, for example, they say pápier. "This patois," says Dr. Brown, "has few inflections to give it expressiveness, but this quality is communicated to it in perfection by a vast variety of modifications of voice and gesture in the person speaking. But one mood, that known among grammarians by the term infinitive, is applied to the verbs, and the differences of time and circumstances are expressed by prefixing the particles before the word. Thus, *je parle* is expressed *moi parler; je parlais* by *moi te parler;* the particles *te* and *va* being corrupt derivations from the auxiliary French verbs *etre* and *aller;* and the phrase signifying literally, — Me speak, Me was spoke, and Me going to speak. It is said that no foreigner is capable of attaining a complete knowledge of all the occult significations and the varied expressions given by the natives to this negro French, by the means of the changes and combinations to which the different phrases are subjected by the speakers. What cannot be expressed in any other language, can be easily uttered or signified through this singular flexibility of the Creole tongue by means of one or two words adroitly selected and accompanied by the peculiar gesture and intonation significant of the idea. This language runs readily into rhyme, and the blacks express both their joy and grief by song; and by a union of singing and pantomime, they mysteriously describe their future designs of insurrection, pillage, or love." To Mr. Bishop I am indebted for the following conjugation of the verb *faire*, as it would be conjugated if the Creole had a grammar:

Indicative.

Faire — To do.

Present.

M'a pé fait * — I am doing.
Ou'a pó fait — Thou art doing.

* This, following Dr. Brown, should be written faire; but as both words are similarly pronounced, I follow Mr. Bishop's manuscript.

L'a pé fait— He is doing.
N'a pé fait— We are doing.
Ou' a pé fait— You are doing.
Y' a pé fait— They are doing.

Imperfect.

M' ta pé fait — I was doing.
Ou ta pé fait— Thou wast doing.
Li ta pé fait—He was doing.
Nou ta pé fait— We were doing.
Ou ta pé fait—You were doing.
Yo ta pé fait—They were doing.

Pas. Déf.

Mon fait, *or* M' té fait—I did.
Ou fait, *or* Ou té fait—Thou didst.
Li fait, *or* Li té fait—He did.
Nou fait, *or* Nou té fait— We did.
Ou fait, *or* Ou té fait—You did.
Yo fait, *or* Yo té fait—They did.

Pas. Ind.

Mon fait—I have done.
Ou fait— Thou hast done.
Li fait—He has done.
Nou fait—We have done.
Ou fait—You have done.
Yo fait—They have done.

Pas. Anté.

M' te fait, &c., &c., &c.

Plus que Parf

M' té fait, &c., &c., &c.

Future.

M' a *or* M' va fait—I will do.
Ou' a *or* Ou va fait— Thou wilt do, &c., &c.

Fut. Ant.

There seems to be no idea, in Creole, answering to—I will have done, except it be the same as the former.*

Condit.

M' ta fait—I would do.
Ou ta fait—Thou wouldst do.
Li ta fait — He would do.

Imper.

Fait—Do thou.
Fait— Do ye, &c.

*M'té va fait, ou té va fait, &c., is the future anterieur.—A. Tate.

The Creole is but little encumbered with rules and tenses. I do not know better how to give the subjunctive than by one or two sentences.

French.

Il veut,
Il exige,
Il désire, } que vous fassiez votre devoir.

Creole.

Li vle,
Li exigé,
Li désiré, } ou fait devoir ou.

French.

Je ne crois pas,
Croyez-vous, } qu' il vienne?

Creole.

M' pas croué,
Esse-ou croué, } l'a vini?

French.

J' ai jugé qu'il dût faire cela.

Creole.

Mon jugé li doit fait ça.

Examples of Phrases.

FRENCH.	ENGLISH.	CREOLE.
Mon père,	My father,	papa-moué.
Ton père,	Thy father,	papa-ou.
Son père,	His father,	papa-li.
Notre père,	Our father,	papa-nou.
Votre père,	Your father,	papa-ou.
Leur père,	Their father,	papa-yo.

French — La Maison de mon père.
Creole — La kaië papa moué.
French — L'ami de son frère.
Creole — Z'ami frê li,
French — L'argent de cet homme.
Creole — L'agent nomme-la.

There is one very expressive word in Creole, used to express anything and everything, and that word is Bagaïe. "Bagaïe moué" means everything belonging to me. Thus: "Li prend bagaïe moué, li pas vlé ba moué li — He has taken something of mine, and he does not wish to give it back." There is one singular way of expressing strongly in Creole, which resembles a Hebrew peculiarity of expression: "Allé m'a pour allé. Literally: "Going, I am going;" or "I am really going." "C'est vlé ou pas vlé — It is wishing you do not wish," or "You really do not wish." "Ou mizé même, cést vini ou sa? You have been very long — are you only just come?" "Ou trompé, c'est joudi mon vini?" "You are mistaken (literally,) is it to-day that I am come?" or "I have been come some time." The même in Creole is very emphatic: "Li aimé même — he really loves." "Li pas té vlé même — he would not consent on any account." All the emphasis in pronunciation is thrown upon the même. "Eh, bien! comment ou (yé)? "Well, how are you?" The usual answer is: "A la volonté maite;" or "à la volanté de Dié."

The Lord's Prayer in Creole.

"Papa-nou, qui n'en ciel; nou 'mandé ou fait nom ou sanctifié; fait règne ou veni, fait la volonté ou fait nen terre comme n'en ciel. Ba nou jourdi la nourriture qui va suffit nou pour la jounée; pardonné nou péché nou, comme nou pardonne ça qui péché conte, nou, pas quitté nou tombé nen tentation mais ouété nou nen main satan. AMEN."

The translation furnished to me by Mr. Ackermann is somewhat different. I subjoin it, also, so that both versions may be compared with the French original: —

"Papa nou, ou qui nen ciel, nom ou li saint, que royaume ou pour nou, et que volonté ou va fait sou terre cou nen ciel. Bah nou di pain 'joudi nou besoin et pardon pour offences nou fait ou, cou nou a pé bay pardon a tout moun qui offensé nou et pas quitté nou tombé nen tentation: mais delivré nou de tout sa qui mal, ce royaume là tout c'est pour vou, par not seigneur. AMEN."

Creole can be acquired easily in three or six months if one lives among the people. In order to facilitate the acquisition of the dialect, a grammar, with conversations, phrases, songs, and the proverbs of Hayti, in Creole, will be issued under the supervision of the Bureau of Emigration.

"With the blacks," says Moreau de St. Mery, writing of Hayti at the close of the last century, "gestures are very numerous, and they form an intrinsic part of their language. They love, above all, to express imitative sounds. Do they speak of a cannon shot, they add *bōūme;* of a musket shot, *poûme;* of a blow on the face, *pîmme;* of a kick, or blow with a stick, *bimme;* of whipping, *v'lap v'lap.* Does one fall down lightly, they add, *bap;* heavy, it is *boum;* in tumbling down, *blôu coutoūm;* and whenever they wish to render an imitative sound, they repeat the term as far, far, far, far away, — which signifies at a great distance."

INDUSTRY.

The chief manufactures of Hayti are syrup, rum, and taffia, which is a kind of unclarified rum, much used by the lower people. The manufacture of brown sugar has recently been commenced. Measures are said to be in progress for the revival of the manufacture of white sugar, which, since the days of the French, has never been a flourishing branch of industry in Hayti. Haytian syrup is of the finest quality, as it contains all the juice, not the mere refuse of the juice of the sugarcane. A variety of preserves are exported. The cities furnish bricklayers, masons, cabinet-makers, carpenters, saddlers, tailors, cordwainers, coopers, tanners that made good sole leather, blacksmiths, goldsmiths, tinsmiths, wheelwrights, and hatters. There are not enough hatters to supply the demand, and, indeed, first-rate, industrious workmen, in any trade, would soon be able to establish themselves. There are no saw-mills in operation in Hayti, no brick-yards, no shingle machines, very few ploughs, and none of our improved agricultural implements. The country offers a large field for their introduction, by persons who will themselves employ them.

The Haytian women excel in all kinds of needlework, in embroidery in silk and cotton, and in the manufacture of wax flowers and fruits.

The Haytian coasters, which are from ten to fifty tons' burthen, are all built by native workmen. The ropes generally used in the country districts are made of palm leaves and hemp ; but fine ropes are also made from the leaves of the great aloe. For domestic purposes water crouches are manufactured of unglazed ware ; and oil, for burning, is extracted from the nut of the Palma-Christi. This is what we call hot-drawn castor oil. The fine arts have several professors at the capital ; and the Palace has many of the best works of Haytian painters. Thè bust of President Geffrard, to be found at the Bureau in Boston, will give an idea of the ability of the Haytian artists in that department of the fine arts.

POPULATION.

The population of the Dominican Republic is generally stated at 120,000; it certainly is not greater, and probably is less. No reliable census of Hayti has been taken since the days of the French; because the country people, having a traditional aversion to such an enumeration, have thrown numerous obstacles in the way of one. Their ancestors associated the census with slavery; and such conjunctions have hitherto been fatal to every governmental project of the kind. The schoolbooks of Hayti state its population at 800,000. But, after a careful study of all the statistics that have been published since the days of the French, and a review of the various causes which have tended to prevent a rapid increase, I cannot see how the present population of Hayti can be more than 600,000. A census has been ordered by the Government; and this point, therefore, will soon be decided. There are not five hundred whites in Hayti.

II.

Notes on Religion and Education.

THE CATHOLIC CHURCH.

THE history of the Catholic religion in Hayti is unique and interesting. Even in the days of the colonists, the power that the Pope wields in other Catholic countries, was never exercised in Hayti; and, since the dawn of the National Independence of the conquering race, that deep-rooted and just jealousy of white domination which led the fathers of the Constitution to confine, forever, to men of African and Indian descent, the right of holding real estate in the Island, has safely guarded the prerogatives that the French formerly enjoyed against all the encroachments of ecclesiastical ambition. Hence, for many years, the Haytian people, although Catholics, have professed no spiritual allegiance to the Pope. The Head of the State has also been the Head of the Church — and the anomaly has been presented of a democratic Catholic church — a church without a bishop or any grade of superior clergy! All, hitherto, have been priests only, receiving their appointment from the State. This independence, however, has not been of unmixed advantage. The necessity of having priests has often compelled the past Governments to appoint any one, qualified to perform the Catholic ceremonies, who presented himself as a candidate for the office. Hence, the unfrocked priests of Europe, and men who left their country for their country's good, have frequently been appointed the spiritual guides of the people. Unprincipled, licentious, and mercenary, these men,—

drunkards, many of them, and living openly with concubines, — having no other interest in the well-being of the people than is implied in the right of receiving their fees, instead of encouraging marriage and discouraging the Vaudoux, and teaching — not only by precept but example — the morality of the Christian religion, have brought discredit on its name, contributed to demoralize their flocks, and united in adding to Obeah rites the ceremonies of the Catholic faith. With a few noble exceptions, this has been the general character of the priests of Hayti. With three or four exceptions, also, these men have been whites,— natives chiefly of Corsica; for the simple country people have a notion that whites only can be efficient *pères*. (Many of them, certainly, in one sense, have been very efficient *pères*.) Under such a state of things, the moral progress of the people must necessarily have been slow. This subject has often occupied the attention of past Governments; but the only remedy — a concordat with the Pope for the purpose of obtaining priests of good repute — has always been an insurmountable obstacle in the way. For the Haytian Ruler has always refused to abdicate his chieftainship; and the Pope, on the other hand, has inflexibly insisted on the absolute control of ecclesiastical affairs. This difficulty has at last been overcome by the concession, on the part of the Pope, of the most liberal concordat that has ever been concluded with the Holy See. It provides that the Bishop shall be appointed by the President, subject to the confirmation of the Pope; and to this Bishop the power shall be given of nominating the priests, subject to the approval of the President. It requires that the bishop and priests shall give an oath of fidelity to the Haytian Government. The concordat has been ratified by the Senate and transmitted to Rome for signature. Under Soulouque, and still, (September, 1860,) there are only about thirty priests in the Republic. There will be seventy when the Concordat is signed and in force. The church in Hayti is supported by the fees paid by its members for the various rites performed; and by a trifling annual contribution made by the Government for the repairs of ecclesiastical edifices. The law fixes the rate of charges for burials and high masses, which are paid to a church-warden *(Marguillier)*, who is a civil officer, and who expends it, under the direction of the Communal Council, for the use of the church — one part to the priest and his assistants, and the rest for vestures, and the other necessities of the Catholic service. The sums paid for baptisms, marriages, and petty masses are the exclusive income of the priest.

PROTESTANTISM.

Protestantism was introduced into Hayti in 1816, by the Wesleyan Methodists of England, at the special invitation of President Pétion; and to the number of their converts were added, in 1821, many of the emigrants under President Boyer. There are now about 1,400 Protestants in the Republic. The English Wesleyan Methodists support four stations; the English Baptists one; and the United States one. They are also two Haytian Protestant churches. The largest liberty is allowed to Protestants in every part of the Republic; and not only the exercise of their faith, but the fullest right to promulgate it is guaranteed by the Government and Constitution of the country.

RELIGIOUS TOLERATION.

Religious toleration is a prominent characteristic of the Haytian people. Although they are Catholics they have never persecuted Protestants. No civilized nation in the world has so stainless a record on this point. The great principle of toleration has been embodied in every Constitution, and maintained under every form of Government that has prevailed in Hayti, from the dawn of its National Independence.

Dessalines, who completed the extinction of the whites, first proclaimed the doctrine of religious toleration.

In the Constitution of 1805 of the Empire of Hayti, the fifteenth article declares that the "laws admit of no governing religion;" the fifty-first, that "the liberty of worship is tolerated;" and the fifty-second, that "the State makes no provision for the support of either worship or minister."

Pétion, the first President of the Republic of Hayti, made equally liberal provisions. In the Constitution of 1806, the thirty-fifth article is, "The Roman Catholic religion being the religion of all the Haytians, is the religion of the State. It shall be specially protected; as, also its ministers." Article 36 is, "The law allows each minister the extent of his spiritual administration. Their ministers cannot, under any pretext, form a body of State." Article thirty-seventh is, "*If, hereafter, other religions are introduced, no person shall be restrained in the exercise of the religion of their choice;* provided he conforms to the laws." I venture the assertion that the statute book of no other nation contains so remarkable a provision,—the assertion of the right of religious freedom by a nation of Catholics only, in anticipation of a possible future contingency.

Protestantism was introduced under Pétion, by his special invitation, in 1817; he gave the missionaries a cordial welcome, and assured them of perfect liberty to preach, travel, and build houses of worship where they pleased.

In the Constitution of 1816, under Boyer, the forty-ninth article reads, "All religious worship is permitted in the Republic, conformably with the laws."

By the Constitution of 1843, (under Reviere,) "All religions are equally free. Each one has the right to profess his religion and worship in freedom; provided he does not disturb the public order."

In the Constitutions of 1846 and 1849, (the last being under the Empire of Soulouque,) the rights of religious freedom and worship are expressed in the language of the Constitution of 1843.

The Constitution of 1846 is in vigor now. The emphatic declaration of the present Government, that "no one shall be called on to defend the Roman Catholic religion, whether he believes it or not,'' and the frequent official repetitions of its intention to permit no manner of religious persecutions, are guarantees that the principle of religious toleration will suffer no abatement under the enlightened rule of President Geffrard and his ministers. Such official guarantees, however, are unnecessary; the character and history of the people are all sufficient. If there are those, however, who desire to make "assurance doubly sure" in this respect, they will find ample opportunities of doing so in the archives of the Bureau at Boston.

EDUCATION.

The colonial slaveholders of Hayti, like the slaveholders in our Southern States, kept their bondmen, as much as possible, in a state of profound ignorance; but, unlike their American fellow-criminals of our day, instead of making merchandise of their illegitimate offspring, they freed and educated them,— often sending them to the academies and colleges of France. Dessalines, the first independent ruler of Hayti, did not encourage education, for he said that the parade ground was the best school for his people, and a musket the fittest text book. Christophe, however, Pétion, and Boyer, pursued a different policy, and established numerous schools in every part of the country. Soulouque did nothing for education; but, both directly and indirectly, encouraged barbarism. The school system withered under his blighting influence. Since the establishment of the present Republic, however, energetic efforts have been made to revive and extend educational institutions.* The old schools have been restored, and many new ones

* "Primary Instruction has made noteworthy progress; the schools founded in the rural sections, since the Revolution, gather together the youth of both sexes. Government proposes to make these schools agricultural. The work of the fields, which, in a few years, will be directed and executed by practical men, will produce important results. Four National Lycées, 89 primary boys' schools, 21 primary girls' schools, 56 rural schools, a girls' boarding-school for the higher branches of instruction, a naval school, a school of medicine, a school of jurisprudence, a school of music, a school of painting, instruct, at the expense of the State, in all the extent of the Republic, 13,000 pupils. In private schools, also, there are a considerable number of young pupils of both sexes."—*Exposition of the General Situation of the Republic*, *Sept.* 27, 1860.

founded. Girls' schools, also, which had not previously existed, have been recently introduced. Much yet remains to be done in this reform; and American emigrants, it is hoped, will give to the Government an energetic aid in accomplishing it. The President informs the editor, (August, 1860,) that there are now twelve thousand children attending the public schools. There are eight weekly newspapers published in Hayti; one at Cape Haytian, one at Cayes, and six at Port-au-Prince.

COPPER COINS OF HAYTI.

III.

Navigation and Commerce.

HITHERTO the science of statistics has been utterly neglected in Hayti. Up to the date of the fall of Soulouque, the official statistics of *all* of the preceding Governments were worse than useless; for they were the result of a deliberate calculation to deceive on the part of their public agents. Under the Empire, for example, the most responsible Custom-House officers received a nominal salary that was barely sufficient to keep them in cigars. Hence, ships heavily laden with French or English goods, which should have paid a duty amounting to thousands of dollars, were often reported in the Government returns as having arrived — *with ballast!* The comptrollers got rich in a few years with the profits of such ballast, and proslavery politicians in America became Gradgrind-Jeremiahs when they wrote about unfortunate Hayti. A different system has been established by Geffrard, but sufficient time has not yet elapsed, owing to other serious and pressing duties, to organize a systematic Bureau of Statistics. The two following articles, however, from the *Travail,* (Port-au-Prince,) of September 16, 1860, are official, and their figures as nearly correct as it is possible to obtain them under existing circumstances. An addition of ten per cent. on all the figures would give very nearly the true result, — thus allowing for the difference between English and Haytian weights and measures, and admitted errors in the returns. The first article is on the commerce between Hayti and the United States:

"The navigation of the United States in Hayti employs, under the American flag, one half of the foreign ships that frequent our ports. As these vessels are generally smaller than those which come from Europe, they represent only forty-two per cent. of the total tonnage. But it should be remarked that, thanks to their full cargoes both in arriving and returning, they can fix their rate of freight at more favorable terms than their competitors. The remark which has almost become an axiom, that the navigation of a people develops itself in proportion to the products exported, finds here a new proof. The value of the importations from the United States, and the amount of the duty paid by them to the treasury, is about forty per cent. of the total. It represents $2,250,000, [worth of imports,] of which ninety per cent. arrive under the American flag. The chief of these importations are pork, in its different forms, and flour, which amount to about fifty per cent. of them. Subjoined are the figures of the quantities introduced, and of the indication of their value:

Candles	$20,000	Soap	215,000
Butter and Cheese	40,000	Articles of which similar are produced in the country:	
Gold and Silver	65,000		
Furniture and Manufactured Wood	25,000	Lumber and Shingles	70,000
Cotton Stuffs	220,000	Rice	110,000
Flour	500,000	Other Articles	65,000
Salt Beef	20,000	Tobacco, in Leaves and Manufactured	150,000
Fish	230,000	Refined Sugar	15,000
Pork, Ham, and Lard	475,000		$2,250,000
Iron	30,000		

"Pork, building woods, tobacco, rice, refined sugar, amount to forty per cent. on the total importation. In proportion as our general industry shall develop itself, the importation of these articles will diminish; for we are quite as well situated as the United States to produce such articles. It is greatly to be desired that our culture of tobacco, rice, and sugar, should be sufficiently advanced in order to exclude from the list of our consumptions the productions of the Southern States of the Union. This reduction, however, would hardly impede our commerce with the United States, whose growth in the arts and manufactures increases every day. What our exchanges would lose on the one side, they would gain on the other; but should our economical principles suffer by it, we would be happy to see our relations, even indirect, with the South, disappear from our commercial tables. We have one regret to express in relation to our navigation,—it is, that our national flag has disappeared from our intercourse with the United States. In 1853, we had twenty entries under the Haytian flag; to-day we have not one. This result is due to the unskilfulness of the Empire which suppressed the additional duty of ten per cent. on the flags of all States that had not representatives at our Capitol. This was not only a disregard of our own interest, but it was a sacrifice, also, of every sentiment of national dignity to admit an American agent here, when a reciprocal right was refused to us at Washington." *

The next article relates to the commerce of Port-au-Prince alone, for the first six months of 1860:

"We are enabled to offer our readers a few remarks on the

* Hayti was the first country, after the United States, that successfully threw off European allegiance. Yet, up to the present time, the independence of Hayti has never been acknowledged by the great American Republic, whose example she was the first to imitate; although France, the mother country, England, Spain, Prussia, Belgium, and all Christendom, have done so,—many of them having ambassadors and consuls in Port-au-Prince, and receiving at their Courts her accredited representatives. We have recognized the independence of every unwashed and ragged-trousered Republic of Central and South America; even, among the number, petty tribes whose kings, as a royal costume, wear a shirt collar, a cigar, and a pair of spurs. We have expensive embassies in a dozen countries, whose united commerce with us does not amount to one half of our annual commerce with Hayti. Soulouque, with imbecile indifference, permitted commercial agents, instead of consuls, to be established in the open ports of his Empire, on condition only that similar agents, on his part, *citizens of the United States*, should be appointed in Boston, New York, and Philadelphia. He abolished, also, the increased duty mentioned in the text. No change has yet been made by the Government of the Republic, but should the result of the approaching Presidential election show that our policy toward Hayti is to be continued, energetic measures, it is said, will at once be taken to curtail and transfer to the more courteous provinces North of us, the large and increasing commerce that we now carry on with her.

commercial activity of Port-au-Prince during the first six months of 1860, as well as the amount of duty collected by the Custom-House of the same port in the same time.

"The import tonnage has risen to 17,865 tons, and the export to 19,860. As usual, the United States hold the first rank, and are represented in the following table by 9,600 tons.

France	5,000 tons.
England	2,200 "

Hanover, Denmark, Sweden, Hamburg, Belgium, Holland, and Spain, complete the list,

"The amount of the invoices of importation is $1,438,145, Spanish.

For the United States	$665,400
For England	343,870
For France	228,680

The countries named above make up the difference.

"The amount of exportation, reduced into Spanish dollars, at the rate of fourteen Haytian dollars to one Spanish, $1,408,000. This comprises:

France	$775,000
United States	275,000
England	190,000

And the other countries.

"The import duties amount to $300,000.

United States	$104,000
France	74,000
England	53,000
Other countries	69,000

"The export duties amount to $275,000.

France	$135,00
United States	46,000
England	33,000
Other countries	61,000

"Exportation comprises the following products:

Coffee	*15,000,000 pounds.
Logwood	8,400,000 "

* Add nearly eight per cent. (7.958) for the difference between Haytian and avoirdupois pounds.

Cotton	93,000 pounds.
Cocoa	685,000 "
Mahogany	88,000 feet.

"The exportation of Coffee in French vessels has amounted to 7,500,000 pounds.

American	2,300,000 pounds.
English	1,835,000 "
Danish	1,060,000 "
Swedish	750,000 "
Other countries	1,555,000 "

"It will be observed on examining the above figures, that the imports and exports are nearly to the same amount, — a fact which, if it were general, would indicate a healthy condition in the commerce of importation.

"As is usually the case, the amount of merchandise coming from France is in proportion neither to the special tonnage of that country nor to the exportation. Thus, for a half-yearly importation of about 1,200,000 francs, France has received in return, 5,000,000 of francs of our produce.

"The difference is explained by the preference given to our Coffee by the French; a preference on which speculators have depended, on the strength of the new law in France; on the other hand, the imports from the United States and England are double the amount of the remittances under their flags. This fact proves that the commerce with America and England has been transacted through drafts on France, and that American vessels, of a tonnage so considerable on the comparative table, have been laden with articles of small value. Indeed, out of 8,400,000 pounds of logwood exported, the United States have taken 6,200,000.

"Another observation worthy of remark is, that for an importation of $228,680, the French have paid $74,000 for import duty, or 33 per cent., and the English for $343,870, have paid only $53,000, or less than 16 per cent. Although the merchandise received from France is often composed of articles of luxury, we think there is occasion to examine the question under its several aspects. Certainly the tonnage duty, weighing according to our system on the imports, modifies the proportion, since on one hand 5,000 tons represent only a value of $228,-680, whilst on the other, 2,200 tons give $343,870. But this circumstance is not sufficient to explain so great a difference. We think it would be good in the interest of the consumer to take these observations into consideration. Many articles which have been long looked upon as things of luxury, are made to-day at very low prices, and would be accessible with a moderate duty, but are excluded from our habits by a heavy tax. However, we reason on existing facts, reserving any discussion on sumptuary taxes. The duty on American cargoes, which are composed, for the most part, of provisions, has been likewise below 16 per cent."

By far the largest portion of the exports and imports occurs in the autumn months of October, November, and December. During the first six months of every year, not more than one third of the annual exports and imports are made. The foregoing figures, therefore, must be regarded in the light of this fact, to give a true result in estimating the yearly commerce of the capital.

So far, for the commerce between the States and Hayti, and for the trade of the chief port. These subjoined figures, which are also official, will give an idea of the general commerce of the Republic: "The exportations of Hayti employ annually between 500 and 600 vessels, giving a total of about 70,000 tons, distributed among the following nations:

	SHIPS.	TONNAGE.
United States	250	30,000
England	90	12,000
France	70	12,000
Germany, Danish, Swedish, Russian	50	8,000
Holland, Belgium, Italian, Central America, Spanish	50	7,000"

To these figures must be added 25 per cent., in order to arrive at their registry tonnage; for the Haytian mode of computation gives invariably between 25 and 30 per cent. less than the ship's register.

"The import duties paid to the State, under the Empire, averaged between $800,000 and $900,000 annually, and were derived as follows:

United States	$300,000
England	190,000
France	190,000
Other Flags	180,000

"The annual exportations of the principal staples may be estimated thus:

Coffee	50,000,000 lbs. Haytian.
Logwood	50,000,000 " "
Cotton	700,000 minimum.
Cocoa	1,200,000 lbs. Haytian.
Mahogany	2,500,000 feet reduced."

IV.

Political Notes.

TERRITORIAL DIVISIONS OF THE REPUBLIC.

POLITICALLY, the Republic is divided into departments; the departments into arrondissements; the arrondissements into communes; and these last into rural sections.

The departments have no commanders-in-chief; but each arrondissement has a commander, who, up to the present time, has always been an officer of superior rank. They receive their orders from the different Secretaries of State, whom they represent in their respective arrondissements; they are the political administrators, and are intrusted with the superintendence of the high police.

Each commune also is commanded by a military officer, who is responsible to the commander of the arrondissement of which the commune forms a part.

The rural sections of the communes are commanded by officers of rural police, who are responsible to the commander of the commune.

There are five departments, to wit, the departments of the South, the West, the Artibonite, the North and Northwest.

There are twenty-one arrondissements, viz: Cayes, Tiburon, Grand'Anse, Nippes, Aquin, Jacmel, Léogane, Port-au-Prince, Mirebalais, Lascahobas, St. Mark, Gonaïves, Marmelade, Môle, St. Nicholas, Port de Paix, Borgne, Cape Haytian, Limbé, Grande Rivière, Trou, Fort Liberté. There are fifty-five communes.

For the administration of justice, the territory of the Republic is divided into seven civil jurisdictions, which also, as has been already seen, takes cognizance of criminal, correctional, and maritime or admiralty cases, to wit, the jurisdiction of Cayes, Jérémie, Jacmel, Port-au-Prince, Gonaïves, Cape Haytian, and Port de Paix.

The civil tribunals have their sittings in these towns, — the chief places of the jurisdiction. The tribunals of Commerce also have their sittings in them, and extend their jurisdiction over the same divisions.

The tribunal of Cassation sits in the capital.

Each commune has a Police Court, (Tribunal de Paix,) the jurisdiction of which extends over the commune.

For the administration of Finances, the territory is divided into ten financial arondissements, to wit, Cayes, Aquin, Jérémie, Nippes, Jacmel, Port-au-Prince, St. Mark, Gonaïves, Port de Paix, Cape Haytian. The administrators reside in these towns, the ports of which are the only ones opened to foreign commerce.* They have under their orders, the respective treasurers, the directors of customs, and the Government storekeepers; and besides, the Government overseers, who, in the communes, hold all the administrative functions.

STATE REVENUE AND DEBTS.

The State Revenues are drawn from the duties on exports and imports, harbor dues, stamps, registry fees, the sales and leases of public lands and buildings, and the "patents" or licenses of merchants. The State income averages over $2,000,000 per annum. Of this amount about $800,000 are derived from the tax on coffee. The import duties range between $900,000 and $1,200,000.† An immense future income will probably be derived from the exploitation of the woods, islands, and mines of the Republic. The National Debt contracted for the "Indemnity," and a loan from France, amounts

* The open port of Nippes is Miragoâne; the other towns bearing also the names of the arrondissements.

† In 1860, the Custom-House of Port-au-Prince alone yielded $700,000 of import duties.—A. TATE.

to about $8,000,000; which will be totally extinguished in 1879, by the payments annually made according to the treaty. The paper money in circulation amounts to between two and three millions of American dollars in value.

ARMY.

Every Haytian has been trained to military duty. The armed force of the nation has always been large. The standing army of the Republic, under Boyer, was 40,000 men; and under Soulouque, shortly before his abdication, it reached 22,000. The history of the country will explain this extraordinary fact, by showing how the maintenance of the national Independence, and the rivalries of rulers, have seemed to render a numerous armed body indispensable. The reduction of this force to the lowest possible point, is a reform that every patriot desires to see accomplished, and one which the present administration is rapidly achieving. The army has already been reduced to 10,900 men. It is thus organized and divided:

32 regiments of Infantry - - - - -	6,400 men.
4 regiments of Artillery - - - - -	1,000 "
8 Corps de Garde - - - - - -	3,000 "
Cavalry - - - - - - - - -	500 "
	10,900 "

The police, which is also an armed body, numbers 3,100 men.

Not more than one half of the army is engaged in duty at the same time; for it is otherwise organized than the forces of the United States. "The armed force," says a Haytian author, "is divided into the paid National Guard and the unpaid National Guard. The first class includes all those who live under the rule of military discipline; the second class, every one capable of bearing arms, — which the law makes the duty of all men between the ages of fifteen and sixty years. Ordinarily, but a very small number of the soldiers, (the first class,) are in service each week in their respective garrisons or cantons, while the rest are left at liberty to work at their respective industrial occupations, and particularly at the cultivation of the fields; but, at the slightest indication of danger, these soldiers rush spontaneously to their colors. The unpaid National Guard drills on the first Sunday of every month, and are reviewed in the communes in which they reside. In case of war they join the military force, and are actively associated with them. The commanders of arrondissements have under their order the National Guard of their respective arrondissements; at their requisition they formed themselves, for the trial of military offences, into special councils, which assembled at the chief towns of the arrondissements."

The police receive seven Haytian dollars weekly; the common soldiers, two dollars, for rations, and an occasional small bounty; the President's Body Guard, (Les Tirailleurs,) two dollars a day, with rations and clothing. In 1859, the expense of the army, including the police, amounted to $555,000 Haytian; by the last reduction in numbers, it will cost $350,000 for the present year. Still further reductions will be made in future.

NAVY.

The navy of Hayti, under Soulouque, consisted of six small vessels, which were used for the purpose of transporting provisions, prisoners, soldiers, or messages from port to port. It is now suppressed. Two steam vessels — "The Geffrard," and "The 22d of December" — made in France, have been substituted for it.

LAWS.

The laws of Hayti consist of the provisions of the "six codes," which, with some modifications, are a copy of the Code Napoleon. The six codes were published in 1825. The laws passed since that time have not been yet codified. The President, in certain prescribed cases, has the power of making provisional enactments, "Arrêtés," which are in force until the meeting of the Chambers; when, if the Legislative bodies ratify them, they become statute laws; if not, they lose their efficacy. (See Constitution.) Before a law, passed by the Chambers, is enforced, it must be proclaimed by authority of the President. This proclamation is made by a public reading of the law by a military company in every city, town, village, and commune in the Republic.

CURRENCY.

It is the peculiar maxim of Haytian merchants that gold is merchandise; fluctuating in value like other articles of commerce. That is to say, the relation that gold (called *monnaie forte* or *piastres)* bears to the currency of the country, (or *monnaie nationale,)* is subject to the ordinary changes of trade. The entire retail commerce of the country is carried on in national money, of which the standard is the *gourde*, sometimes also called the Haytian dollar. At different times of the year the value of the *piastre* ranges at from twelve to sixteen gourdes; but in seasons of political trouble, as when the Revolution was progressing, it has even reached nineteen. The most noteworthy fact connected with the national currency is, that it chiefly consists of paper money,—bills, of about twice the size of American bank notes, of one and two gourdes in value. When the rate of exchange, or, as they say in Hayti, the value of the piastre, is as one to twelve, a gourde is worth 8¼ cents American currency; and a bill of two gourdes, therefore, 16½ cents. There are also metallic coins,—four gourdes, two gourdes, one gourde, and half a gourde, in silver-alloyed pieces; and the one gourdine, (¼ gourde,) the gros cob, (of which there are 12 in a gourde,) and the petit cob, (of which there are 24,) of copper. The value of one gros cob and one petit cob, is called an *escalin*, of which eight would make a gourde; but, like the pence and shillings of New England, there is no coin of the name. Twelve French pounds weight of copper money is worth a hundred Haytian dollars. You can do nothing in the retail and internal trade with gold in Hayti. It is only the wholesale importing business of the country that takes cognizance of piastres and doubloons. The coins of Hayti have national stamps.*

HAYTIAN WEIGHTS AND MEASURES.

The old French weights and measures are the standards of Haytian weights and measures, as follows:

WEIGHT.

Haytian.	American Avoirdupois pounds.	Kilos, modern French.
1 lb.	= 1.0795854	= 0.4895
2 "	= 2.1591708	= 0.9790
3 "	= 3.2387562	= 1.4685
4 "	= 4.3183416	= 1.9580
5 "	= 5.3979270	= 2.4475
10 "	= 10.795854	= 4.8950
100 "	= 107.95854	= 48.9500

LINEAR OR LONG MEASURE.

Haytian.	American.	French.
1 foot	= 1.065636 feet.............	= 0.3248 mêtres.
2 feet	= 2.121272 "	= 0.6596 "
3 "	= 3.196909 "	= 0.9744 "
4 "	= 4.262545 "	= 1.3192 "
5 "	= 5.328181 "	= 1.6240 "
10 "	= 10.656363 "	= 3.2480 "
100 "	= 106.563632 "	= 32.4800 "

* The pieces bear the denomination of 1 gourde; 50 cents; 25 cents; and 12½ cents, silver coins. 6 cents; 2 cents; 1 cent, copper. In 1852 the value of all Haytian metallic coins was raised fourfold, thereby bringing them up to their intrinsic value, with a view to prevent the very extensive exportation of them, which was illicitly carried on, and left a handsome profit to the smuggler.—C. H. B.

SUPERFICIAL OR SQUARE MEASURE.

Haytian.		American sq. ft.		American sq. yd
One carreau, or the square on a base of 350 Haytian feet, or 372.97259832 American feet	=	139108.56035076	=	15456.50670
2 carreaux	=	278217.12070150	=	30913.01340
3 "	=	417325.68105228	=	46369.52010
4 "	=	556434.24140300	=	61826.02680
5 "	=	695542.80175360	=	77282.53350
10 "	=	1391085.6035076	=	154565.06705
100 "	=	13910856.035076	=	1545650.67056

100 " equal 319.34931 acres; 1 carreau equals 3.1935 acres.

1 carreau equals 12913.1424 French square mêtres.

LIQUID MEASURE.

Haytian gallon equals, 231 cubic inches, English.
or, 0.833111 Imperial gallon, English.
or, 3.78520 French litres.

1 French litre equals 61.027051313 cubic inches, English.

Haytian gallon equals 3 quarts and nearly ⅓, or 3.332444 quarts.

LEGAL RIGHTS OF WHITES.

The legal rights of the white race in Hayti are not very numerous. They cannot possess real estate, nor hold mortgages for longer than nine years; they cannot become citizens, and, consequently, can neither vote nor attain political position; if they marry Haytian women, even, they cannot inherit their landed property, but only the proceeds of it when sold at a public action. They can be wholesale merchants, artists, mechanics, professors, teachers, clerks, engineers, and the lessees of estates; but the retail trade, the bar, and the bench, military honors and civil distinctions have not been placed within the scope of their attainment. In social life, however, and in the callings for which they are legally qualified, they are treated with all the courtesy and regard to which their character entitles them. Exemplary conduct on their part always enables them to overcome the social disadvantages attaching to their unfortunate color.

THE HAYTIAN EMBLEMS.

As the Coat of Arms of Hayti will be found in the title-page, it is unnecessary to describe it. The Haytian flag is truly significant: it is the French flag *with the colors reversed and the white element stricken out.* It consists of two colors horizontally placed, the red beneath the blue.

SILVER COINS OF HAYTI.

V.

Diseases of Hayti and their Remedies.

THE catalogue of diseases in Hayti does not present anything nearly so complex in character, nor so many varieties of types, as are known to exist in colder latitudes, and in countries where annually the four seasons succeed each other more uniformly, and where each in particular is characterized by sudden thermometric fluctuations and meteorological transitions. In the maritime towns, and in marshy situations near the seacoast, during the hot months, and also towards the fall of the year, remittent, bilious-remittent, or inflammatory remittent, typhus, and simple continued fevers, and intermittents of the *tertian* type, usually prevail.

An attack from any one form of these fevers is more or less serious, if not decidedly dangerous; the intensity, character, and termination, are always influenced, as in other hot countries, by the habits and temperament of the patient's body, as well as by the nature of the locality where the disease originates.

Individuals of sober, regular habits, who are cleanly in their persons, and whose constitutions are not injured by the use of spirituous liquors and other excesses, may live in Hayti to an advanced age without having been subjected to many serious attacks of fever, or other malignant malady; and this remark applies even to the white or European resident, who is evidently much more predisposed to fall under the evil effects of hot climates, and is more obnoxious to the diseases of torrid countries, than persons of African blood.

The *typhus icterodes*, or yellow fever of the West Indies, may be considered to be a remittent-bilious, inflammatory fever, of insidious typhoid tendency, and is most intolerant towards the unacclimated white blood of Northern countries; its malignity is to be dreaded, most especially by those of plethoric, ardent, and irritable habits. The strong and vigorous, the uncleanly and intemperate, are most liable to the disease, when they fall under its influence in the West Indies.

Of the several maritime, commercial ports of Hayti, that of Port-au-Prince has acquired great notoriety on account of the predominance there of the yellow fever at certain periods. This is not to be denied. But there are aggravating circumstances connected with it that have been seldom examined and classed as such, if not the primary exciting causes of the sickness which so often prevails among foreign shipping in the harbor of Port-au-Prince, as well as in the ports of some other islands, reputed to be equally the seats of yellow fever. The foreign vessels that frequent annually this harbor, with the exception of two or three regular traders, acting as packets, are all of the worst class, in respect to those arrangements necessary to preserve health in a hot country. They are most unwholesome, generally, in their interior conditions, — the pervading atmosphere of their holds, or lower-decks, being essentially mephitic. Such vessels, for the most part, are taken up, no doubt, more on account of the cheapness of freight, than of their sanitary condition; in addition to which, they are managed by mariners of different nations, who habitually are filthy in their persons, reckless, and most intemperate in character and habits, and whose quarters on shipboard, and mode of living in them, are better calculated to engender than to prevent disease within the tropics. If, besides this, we notice with regard to their manner of clothing, and kind and quality of food, that nothing is changed from what they were in frigid climates, it will scarcely be a matter of surprise that so many of that class of men fall victims when attacked by febrific diseases, and when placed in situations in the West Indies favorable to the development of the yellow fever.

It might appear strange when it is known that, even during the period of yellow-fever epidemic, the malady is usually confined to the harbor, and among the mariners and strangers on board foreign vessels; the natives enjoy perfect immunity. This form of fever does not attract attention in the town, otherwise than when sailors and others, who have been seized by it on shipboard in the harbor, are carried on shore for treatment or interment.

During *twenty* odd years' practice in Hayti, I cannot recollect having treated a black person, or one of color of near affinity in blood to the African, who has died in Hayti from black vomit. I have treated many such persons attached to vessels in various capacities, and whose places of birth were reported to be the United States, and different ports in British North America. The blacks were attacked by yellow fever in the same manner as their white shipmates, but in no case has the malady been so deadly with them as with the others; their recovery was quicker, — no black vomit, to my recollection, occurred. Hence, it may be said that the black and colored person, as above stated, natives of cold latitudes, may certainly fall under the influence of the fevers of this country, particularly if imprudent and intemperate in their habits; but that, with certain rare exceptions, the attack will be comparatively less virulent than with the white person. And this is so true, that owners and captains of ships trading to the West Indies and to Hayti, have preferred to have a black or colored crew, rather than a white one, whenever they can procure one. This harbor has been free from epidemic yellow fever since 1857. Not a single case of black vomit has occurred since then.

With this brief exposition of the nature of fevers common to Hayti, and of the influence which they may exercise on those of the African race who may emigrate to this country, it will be seen that they have little to fear from the effects of its climate, and other matters being favorable to all such as like to come over, the question in respect to their health after they shall have arrived, is not less satisfactory. It might even, perhaps, not be irrational to infer that the climate of the tropics would be more salutary and propitious to the greater part, if not to all, without distinction, than that of the so much colder region now inhabited by them in North America, and which does not appear to have been originally strictly destined by nature for the constitution of the African people.

We have shown that sickness is restricted almost to the maritime towns, and to marshy situations in the vicinity of the sea-coast, where it will not be to the interest of emigrants to remain when they get here. We have now to affirm that, away from the towns, in the interior and rural districts, but few diseases or distempers are known; indeed, the interior of the country is so healthful as not to be at all the physician's El Dorado. Members of the profession do not get rich in Hayti. People do die out in the country, as they must die everywhere, but it is seldom or rarely we hear talk of any illness of a complicated or alarming character, such as is common in America and elsewhere.

During the cool or rainy seasons, one will meet with cases of colds, simple catarrhal affections, sore throat, some looseness of the bowels, arising from the use of crude fruits and change of water, which are easily remedied by removal of the causes that incite them; while in the hot, dry season, in certain situations, sore eyes, in its simple form, and deranged stomachs, may also be met with, as in other countries, and which are regarded in country places as of little importance.

We will finish this paper by subjoining a list of simple medicines, which will be useful to the emigrants who are destined, on their arrival in Hayti, to seek their fortunes by locating themselves in the rich, rural, and agricultural districts, at a distance from efficient medical aid, — and for this reason especially we at the same time recommend to all who may decide on coming over, to have themselves and their children vaccinated without fail. These, then, are the simple medicines which families may want, and which they are counselled to bring with them:

½ oz. Sup. Carbonate Soda.
½ oz. Sulph. Quinine.
1 oz. Turkey Rhubarb.
1 oz. Pulvis Jalap.
½ lb. Cream of Tartar.
¼ lb. Calcined Magnesia (in bottles).
1 lb. Epsom Salts.
A little Boneset.
2 oz. Spt. Hartshorn.
2 drachms Extract Opium.
2 oz. Spt. Peppermint.

These different articles will be used according to circumstances, by families whose interest it will be to live out in the country. They should have the *doses* marked on each *packet* or *phial*. And thus we take leave of this subject for the present.

W. G. Smith, M. D.

Port-au-Prince, September 22, 1860.

VI.

Seaports of Hayti.

THE seaports of Hayti rather unfavorably impress the traveller who has never previously visited the West India Islands or Central American States. From various causes, — earthquakes, chiefly, and fires, the indifference of past governments, and the want of proper workmen, — they do not present that aspect of prosperity and neatness which distinguish our Northern cities or the towns of the British American Provinces. The streets are ill-paved, and seldom indicate the scavenger's care; and the stores and private dwellings very plainly show that the art of house-painting has not attained its last perfection.

Port-au-Prince, the capital, is a city of 26,000 inhabitants. It is the seat of Government, and consequently the residence of the President and his ministers; the place where the high courts of justice and the legislative bodies meet. It is the chief port and largest city of the Republic. It has the most sultry climate of all the cities in the Island; yet at Furcy, only eighteen miles distant, there are forests of pines, and a temperature suited for the growth of all the trees and vegetables of the temperate zones.

Cape Haytian, or Cape Hayti, *(Cap Haytien,)* is a town of six or seven thousand inhabitants. It was the capital of the kingdom erected by Christophe, and was formerly known as the Little Paris of the Antilles. It was destroyed by an earthquake in 1842, which occasioned the death of five or six thousand persons, by the fall of the houses and the subsequent fires. There are acres of these ruins still there, — beautifully decorated with luxuriant vegetation. Within a day's ride distant from "the Cape," as it is usually called, are the Citadel and Palace of Christophe, — the most wonderful structures in Hayti, and the greatest architectural triumphs of the colored race. Every visitor should see them. The great Plain of the North, of which Cape Haytian is the port, is unexhaustibly fertile and adapted to every kind of tropical staples.

Port de Paix has a population of about 2,000 inhabitants. It is healthy and well situated, has a good port and a fine country behind it. During the Empire it was a closed port, but it was opened to commerce by the Republic.

Mole St. Nicholas is a closed port. It is a great military point, and was the last place evacuated by the English during their residence in the Island. It is not suited for emigrants; as the country behind it is barren and rocky. Its population is between 1,200 and 1,500.

Gonaïves is a town of 6,000 or 7,000 inhabitants. It is one of the most thriving towns in Hayti. Its commerce is considerable; derived, chiefly, from its exports of dye-woods and mahogany. The plain in which it is situated is admirably adapted to the cultivation of cotton. It was from this town that Toussaint L'Ouverture was kidnapped.

St. Mark, at the further extremity of the same plain, and the scene of many desperate battles, has a population of two or three thousand persons. It is beautifully situated, — very healthy, and with a mild climate. It is the outlet of the great Plain of the Artibonite, — one of the best localities for emigrants in the Island. Two or three hundred Louisiana exiles have already settled there and are highly pleased with the country. There are among them some of the richest colored planters of Louisiana. The Plain of the Artibonite, which extends from the Gros Morne of Gonaïves to the Gros Morne of St. Mark —

a distance of forty-five miles, — and from the Bay sixty miles inland, has no superior, anywhere, for the cultivation of cotton, sugarcane, and tobacco; while the neighboring mountains of Cahos produce some of the best coffee in the Island. There are thousands of carreaux of vacant land in this magnificent tract of country.

L'Arcahaie is a little town of two thousand inhabitants, (thirty-six miles from Port-au-Prince,) and is the centre of a settlement of American emigrants who arrived under Boyer. The surrounding country nearly monopolizes the supply of vegetables for Port-au-Prince. It is not an open port.

Miragoâne, recently opened to commerce, distant seventy miles from the Capital, has one of the best ports in the Island, and is rapidly increasing in importance. A considerable proportion of the American vessels, that discharge at Port-au-Prince, go there to take in cargoes of coffee and dyewoods. The country behind it is mountainous and adapted for the culture of coffee.

Jérémie has a population of three or four thousand. Coffee and sugar are the staple cultures. It is a healthy town, carries on a considerable commerce, and is the outlet of a fertile district. The culture of cotton has recently been recommenced there.

Jacmel is a city of six or seven thousand inhabitants. It has a beautiful bay, somewhat like that of St. Mark, with the similar disadvantage of not having a breakwater, or adequate protection against storms. The country around Jacmel is suited for coffee and dyewoods, of which very large exports are annually made. The British Royal Mail Steamers stop at Jacmel on their passage from Southampton to Jamaica, and also on their return voyages, for the passengers and mails.

Cayes has a similar country near it in producing dyewoods, sugarcane, and coffee in large quantities. The best rum in the Island is made at this town, and it is manufactured on a large scale. It is not exported, but used for home consumption only.

Cape Haytian, Jérémie, Cayes, and Port-au-Prince, export also a large amount of cacao.

The limits of this volume do not permit us to allude to the inland towns and villages.

SILVER COINS OF HAYTI.

VII.

How to Go, and What to Take.

HOW to go and what to take to Hayti, so evidently depends on the position, geographical as well as pecuniary, of the emigrant, that it is not practicable to make this, to every one, a satisfactory chapter. Correspondence with the Haytian Bureau of Emigration in Boston, however, will enable the reader to supply the deficiencies of the Guide.

Some general hints are all that we need give here.

First, as to going. Vessels will sail as frequently as a sufficient number of passengers are procured from Boston and New Orleans. Emigrants from the South will be obliged to defray all the expenses of their passage; as it is not possible, for the moment, to make satisfactory arrangements with vessels from that part of the country. In Hayti, however, this disadvantage will be compensated. An Agent of the Government will be stationed at New Orleans to protect the interests of emigrants. All Southern emigrants, as well as those from the North, are advised to correspond with the Central Bureau at Boston, before selecting a vessel, and the latest information will be sent to them, fully and promptly, and without cost. Passengers will be required to carry their own food for the voyage, or pay for their board for the trip before starting. Those who prefer to provision themselves will be required to have the necessary tin utensils for holding water, drinking, eating, and cooking.

For clothing, take as many summer suits as you can afford to buy; for every kind of manufactured goods is dearer in Hayti than in the United States. Light-colored linen or cotton clothing is the best; with high-crowned straw or Panama hats. Those who design to cultivate coffee, and will, therefore, live in the high lands, will need woollen clothing and blankets; for it is often quite chilly in the ***mornes*** of Hayti. Every one should wear flannel undershirts always. Sheetings, mosquito nettings, all kinds of female costume, and of household wear, — such as tablecloths, towels, and the like,—may advantageously be taken by the emigrant.

Furniture, unless it is old, and will not pay the expense of transportation to the port of shipment, should also be taken out; for chairs, and the finer kinds of furniture, crockery, cutlery, water-coolers, mirrors, glassware, earthenware, and tinware, are very much higher in the West Indies everywhere than in the United States. Glass for windows, and carpets, are not needed. Sofas in plush or haircloth are too hot for comfort; the emigrant should purchase cane-bottomed chairs, and sofas or seats.

Take all your books with you; for English books can seldom be had either for love or money. Take your stationery, also.

You will be allowed to enter, free of duty, provisions enough to last you for two or three months. While you will not be permitted to take advantage of this guarantee to import provisions *for sale*, you should not fail, if possible, to avail yourself of it for the purposes of legitimate consumption. Soap, fish, pork, candles, oil, and salt beef, should be your main articles.

Take such carpenters' tools as you will need. Every family ought to have a saw, hammer, and nails.

Take all the agricultural implements you will require, — handcarts, yokes, ploughs, shovels, rakes, hoes, spades, harness, saddles, churns, and hives.

Washing-machines, tubs, and sewing-machines would be invaluable for your women folk ; for you can buy none of these useful allies of the housewife in Hayti.

Take the best varieties of all kinds of seeds. If you wish to import blooded cattle, or fine breeds of horses, swine, or poultry, the Bureau of Boston will facilitate your object, by making with you advantageous terms of transportation.

VIII.

A Parting Word.

To the Blacks and Men of Color in America:

IN the preceding pages you have been enabled to see — "as in a glass, darkly" — the history of your race in its sole American possession; how rich in every kind of natural wealth that terrestrial paradise is; the character of its people, the nature of its Government, and, by the official papers appended to the Constitution, the disposition of its present Administration.

The voice of history is the voice of God.

Do we not hear it in the existing Black Code of America, and in the acts of the Government of Hayti? Is not the same command of the Still Small Voice, once given to the Chosen Nation, ages before the Christ was born, again thus repeated to His persecuted children in the States, — COME OUT OF HER, MY PEOPLE?

There is a profound significance in the fact of the diversity of races, — far deeper than many of our sages know. It was for a wise and grand purpose that the European and the African have for a time become different in destiny and in physical capacity; and it belongs to the same blind and false philosophy that disputes about the relative superiority of the sexes, to inquire whether the Black man or the White is the more capable of a glorious future. Their missions in the world are different; and, until these are fulfilled, their identity must be preserved.

Has the Black accomplished his destiny in America?

I think that in North America he has; for he is threatened with extinction there. His future is — *annihilation*. There is no other possible result, — whether slavery or freedom shall prevail. Ten men against one, — the contest is decided. Whether at the end of two or of ten generations, the solution of the problem is still, — *annihilation*. Too strong to perish beneath the white man's lash, the black race here will disappear in his arms. Even the pride of giving birth to a new race will be denied to him; for the disproportion, daily becoming greater, between the Blacks and the Whites, gives the future also to the ruler of to-day.

To preserve the African race in America, emigration from it is the first condition. Everything conspires to promote it. Pride of race, self-respect, social ambition, parental love, the madness of the South, the meanness of the North, the inhumanity of the Union, and the inclemency of Canada, — all say to the Black and the man of color, Seek elsewhere a home and a nationality.

I have spoken of the motives arising from a pride of race,— but is it necessary to show you why self-respect, also, repeats and enforces the same advice? When even the churches of the "Founder of Democracy" are closed against you, — and solely because of your race, — why allude to the heathenism which displays itself in your exclusion from the theatres, the omnibuses, and the parlors of the country? I have often heard it said, that with time this prejudice will disappear. *Perhaps*, — but not unless, by an insurrection, successfully conducted, the millions now enslaved exhibit their equality, in courage and in arms, with their masters. The Saxon race is a race of fighters, — its real religion is an evangel of pluck; to men, long-suffering, slow to anger, who return a kiss for a blow, patient and enduring to the end, it exhibits no compassion. Have not the slaves, for two centuries, exhibited these Christian qualities? No man denies it. And yet, what is the opinion that these traits have created in the hearts of the majority of the nation? Two words give it: "*Damned niggers.*" Is there anything yet that points to the result that our prophets predict? Have you not already produced eminent men, — able writers, physicians, and orators? And yet, what has their genius hitherto availed them? I once heard of a distinguished lecturer, who, refused a seat in a first-class car, paid his passage as freight, and was charged by his weight. It was told as a good joke. I think there are two centuries between such jests and equality; and, in the mean time, you will have disappeared from the earth! It is sometimes said that you should remain and fight the battle here, — force a recognition by your genius, industry, character, wealth; teach America to see, in other words, that in you it possesses an invaluable strength. Morality, so exalted, is surely to be admired; but a lower standard, I take it, will do well enough for this world. What are the Americans to you, that you should thus continue to heap benefits on them? You have faithfully served them for nearly two centuries, — denying them nothing, charging them nothing; neither the fruits of your labors nor the fruits of your loins have you withheld; and you have asked in return only enough to eat and the coarsest attire. It is time, now, that you should help yourselves.

There is yet another thing to be considered, that is seldom thought of in urging such a contest,— the casualties of warfare: that where one conquers, ten fall; where one asserts, nine submit; that the voice of prejudice is far oftener the death-knell than the bugle-note of manhood.

Parental love! The schools of New England and other States are open to your children, and they can now receive the advantages of a liberal education. And then? Rendered sensitive by this culture, what prospect is opened to them? A long, petty war with mean men, a fruitless assault on the citadel of place, political and social. Even lions lose their strength in fighting mosquitoes, and such is the warfare to which your children are destined. It is a noble spectacle to see the fight that some brave men among you maintain against the prejudices of Americans, but —

"In vain, alas! in vain, ye gallant few!"

are all your efforts, in behalf of your native land; you are trying to drive back an ocean, which, by its mere physical superiority, will throw up the bodies of your children, after a generation or two, pale and unrecognizable, on its Saxon shores!

In Hayti, a far different future is opened to the colored race. There, it can develop itself in freedom; there, exhibit its capacity and genius. Nowhere else is there such an opportunity presented, — absolutely nowhere in the world.* In Africa, the various races are still separate and hostile; in Hayti, they are all represented and united. The black Haytian, therefore, is the result of the mingling of all of the African bloods; and in him, as is the case with other families of men, this union has produced the best specimen of the race. The men of color there, also, in point of intelligence, ask no favors in any comparison between themselves and their ancestors.

But still another element is needed in Hayti, — the Saxon character, which the men of African descent, to a greater or less extent, in the United States and the Canadas, possess.

She invites this element to come to her. She offers you a home, a nationality, a future. She presents to you the opportunity of not only exhibiting the capacity of your race, but of creating a new Eden in the most fertile of the Antilles; and, at the same time, of checking the Slave Labor System of the South at its source, — in the markets that support it. Would you fight Virginia with a weapon that she will fear as much as she dreaded the rifles of John Brown? Grow tobacco in Hayti,

* Liberia, if a success, will be the white man's victory, for he called it into being, and has fostered it from its birth.

then, and fight her with it on the Liverpool Exchange. Would you retaliate on the Carolinas the punishment that they have often inflicted on your friends? The way is open. Tar and cotton them in England. Hayti will enable you to do it by producing both staples, and hemp enough to boot to hang every friend of Slavery in Missouri and Kentucky. Hayti, which could produce sugar enough to drive Louisiana out of every market in the world; which could raise cotton enough every year to corrupt the morals of a hundred generations of American politicians; which could raise rice enough to bury Wilmington, Charleston, and Savannah out of sight; which, if properly and scientifically cultivated, could raise coffee enough to supply all the wants of Christendom, — Hayti, the home of the Black race, the only country in which it has successfully competed in arms against the Slavery to which Europe condemned, and in which America has held it, invites you, common children of her ancient Motherland, to become a part of her household, and share equally with her own sons the destiny which the Almighty Overruler has marked out from the beginning for her and for you!

May your answer be inspired by wisdom and a spirit of religious consecration!

For myself, firmly believing this work — which, dual in its nature, seeks at once the regeneration of one of the most beautiful Islands of our globe, and the elevation and perpetuity, or, rather, the creation of a coming race, adapted to it and worthy of it—to be one of the most noble and holy enterprises to which any man of our age can be called on to devote his energies and his talents, I accepted the trust confided to me by the Government of Hayti, with a feeling of gratitude to Heaven, which, I trust, will bless with its favor this project for extending civilization, and a true religion, and establishing justice in the Western World.

James Redpath.

INDEX.

BOOKS BY JAMES REDPATH.

I.

THE PUBLIC LIFE OF CAPTAIN JOHN BROWN. By JAMES REDPATH. With an Autobiography of his Childhood and Youth. Boston: Thayer & Eldridge, 114 & 116 Washington Street. 1860. With an accurate steel portrait and illustrations. Handsomely bound in muslin. pp. 408. Price $1.

This volume has been the most successful of the season,—having already reached its FORTIETH THOUSAND, and the demand still continuing very large. It has also been republished in England, and widely noticed by the British press. The *Autobiography* (of which no reprint will be permitted) has been universally pronounced to be one of the most remarkable compositions of the kind in the English language. In addition to being *the* authentic biography of John Brown, and containing a complete collection of his celebrated prison letters—which can nowhere else be found—this volume has also the only correct and connected history of Kansas, — from its opening for settlement till the close of the struggle for Freedom there, — to be found in American literature, whether periodical or standard. It treats, therefore, of topics which must be largely discussed in political life for many years. A handsome percentage, *on every copy sold*, is secured by contract to the family of Capt. Brown. This percentage amounted to nearly $1,800 on the first six months' sale; and will reach $2,000 by the conclusion of the first year of publication. This Volume will be sent by mail, prepaid, to any part of the United States or Canadas, on receipt of the retail price.

Indorsement of the Family of Captain Brown.

The following is an extract from a letter, published in the Conneaut (Ohio) Reporter, by John Brown, Jr., previous to the publication of the Life:

" From a long acquaintance with Mr. Redpath, I consider him not only one of our ablest writers, but from his true appreciation of my father's character, and his intimate acquaintance with him in Kansas, he is probably as well prepared as any one could be to write his history. No danger or hardship prevented his being an eyewitness of the stirring scenes which made so large a part of the history of Kansas. He, like William Phillips, the *Tribune's* Kansas correspondent, seemed to be endowed with the capacity of being omnipresent, and would rush into the jaws of death in pursuit of a fact. To a clear and vigorous mind he adds an honest, faithful, and fearless heart. He is doubtless best qualified to bring out, in their true light, those qualities which are most highly appreciated by the lovers of romance and thrilling incident."

The following joint letter was sent to the Publisher immediately after the publication of the Biography:

North Elba, New York, January, 1860.

We, the undersigned, members of the family and relatives of the late John Brown, desire to express our approval and indorsement of the biography of our honored and revered relative, written by James Redpath, and recently published by Thayer & Eldridge, of Boston, Massachusetts. We think the work the best that can be produced on the subject at the present time; and in all matters of fact, it is essentially correct, while it is written with an enthusiasm and an eloquence which we thoroughly appreciate and admire. The publishers have issued the work in a style which recommends itself to all lovers of a handsome book, in regard to engravings, paper, printing, and binding; and the friends of John Brown who wish to procure and preserve a memorial of his life and deeds, will do well to provide themselves with a copy of this publication.

Mary A. Brown, (Widow of John Brown.)
Salmon Brown,
Isabel Brown,
Henry Thompson,
John Brown, Jr.,
Annie Brown,
Martha Brown,
Abbie C. Brown,
Sarah Brown,
Frederick Brown, (Brother of John Brown.)

Notices of the Press.

"A beautiful printed volume, compiled with great care, by one well acquainted with the subject of its pages."—*Boston Merchants' and Manufacturers' Magazine.*

"Some of it is, no doubt, true, but a larger portion is composed of partisan accounts, garbled extracts, and wilful misrepresentations. Redpath had already provided himself with much of his material in his letters to the New York Tribune from this territory during the disturbances; and where his own store did not supply the venom, he borrows from correspondents as false and truthless as himself. To impeach him and his borrowed authorities is superfluous; a popular verdict has been already rendered against them; and to give an extensive review and exposure of the book is useless, as the readers will perceive its rottenness themselves. But the spirit of the book deserves more than a passing notice. Aside from the fanaticism which marks every page, and which would bring the author to the same gibbet, did he possess the animal courage of Brown, there is a certain studied design in the work to make more "heroes of Harper's Ferry."....Redpath is an abolitionist, hates the Union, is even on the look-out to create sectional strife, and came to Kansas to assist in fomenting civil war between the North and the South, believing the opportunity propitious for bringing about disunion. Such is the biographer of John Brown, and the work was conceived and executed in the same spirit which actuated all his former undertakings. An appeal is directly made to the partisan feeling now existing, — opposing sections are hissed on to strife,— abolition, by servile insurrection, advocated and planned, — John Brown indorsed and canonized,—and the existence of another similar conspiracy divulged."—*Leavenworth* (*Kansas*) *Herald.* [Organ of David R. Atchison.]

"The perusal of it has not only served to fill up a passing hour, but has been the means of conferring much light upon the sufferings of Kansas. The volume is richly interspersed with interesting incidents in the experience of Mr. Brown, which but few beside the author could have given in so graphic, feeling, and touching a manner."—*Protestant Methodist Olive Branch.*

"The author is James Redpath, so prominent in Kansas annals, an intimate, personal friend of Captain Brown, and a spirited and graphic writer. He is probably better adapted to the task than any other person in the country."—*New Bedford Standard.*

"This book is from the vigorous and graphic pen of James Redpath, whose sympathies in the intensely interesting deeds with which he has to deal, is a strong guarantee that this biography will be no ordinary production."—*Marlboro' Mirror.*

"This work is reliable."—*Boston Atlas and Bee.*

"Who can so well write the Life of Osawatomie Brown, as James Redpath, who was with him in Kansas, and fully identified in feeling with the noble object of the old man's life? Had John Brown selected a biographer, James Redpath would unquestionably have been the man."—*Anti-Slavery Bugle.*

"This book will undoubtedly be read by hundreds of thousands. It is written by a friend and admirer. His early history, his Kansas work, his attack on Missouri, and the enterprise in which he lost his life, are all well depicted."—*Zion's Herald.*

"We don't believe in John Brown..... He thought God had called him as a sort of Moses to free the colored race from bondage...... How far this idea is consistent with perfect sanity of mind — *that* is a question not easily solved......We suppose this Life would come within the scope of the "penal act" lately proposed, but it will hardly injure anybody of sound mind."—*Bridgeport* (*Conn.*) *Standard.*

"The author is a writer of ability and experience."—*Williams County Leader* (*Ohio*).

"The tone of the work is that of profound admiration of the subject, and of intense sympathy with the acts for which he lost his life."—*N. Y. Tribune.*

"The reputation of the author of this work, as a writer, and the universal interest taken by the public in the life and character of its subject, rendered the mere announcement of its publication the signal for a demand unparalleled in the history of book publishing....The book is exceedingly well written, and portrays in graphic and faithful colors, the exciting scenes of the Kansas war, the invasion of Virginia, the trial, and the execution." —*Courier, Seneca Falls, N. Y.*

"On the 2d December last, the old man, John Brown, a traitor to the laws of his country, and a high-handed murderer, expiated his treason and his murder on the gallows. There is always a morbid curiosity respecting a noted criminal in the public mind, and this curiosity increases in due ratio to the enormities of which its subject has been guilty. So, John Brown, having planned a wholesale murder, is embalmed in nice white paper and clear type, although his designs were providentially defeated with the sacrifice of but few lives. His biographer, James Redpath, warmly sympathizes with the nefarious scheme of his hero, and being blessed with a wonderful vision, sees promises of future wonder in his early years. He shows us child-Brown, boy-Brown, man-Brown, Kansas-Brown, (a character to be respected, despite the fact that he had a weakness for taking the law in his own hands,) and traitor-Brown.... As a literary production, the book possesses but little merit, being hastily and clumsily executed."—*Chelsea Herald.*

"No better biographer could have been selected, to show the bright side of Captain Brown, than Mr. Redpath. He entered upon his task with his whole soul."—*Boston Transcript.*

"Mr. Redpath's biography is not destitute of merit; but it is so radical in its tone, that it may fail to find that response which it seeks in the breast of the general reader. We are not disappointed in this respect; we know something of the author; he is an impulsive man, but not fickle, and never does things by halves. His book is truthful, and yet somewhat partial. Interesting it is, eminently so; and the author's spirit never flags. The autobiography is one of the most valuable, as it is one of the most entertaining chapters in the volume."—*Woonsocket (R. I.) Patriot.*

"This book is well-written for the purpose for which it was intended,—namely, for inculcating the doctrine that John Brown was a saint and a hero. To the admirers of the leader of the Harper's-Ferry foray, it will doubtless prove very acceptable, as it is in point of literary merit as well as authenticity — so far as the non-political details are concerned — far ahead of any life of the man that has yet been published."—*Providence Post.*

"The accounts of Brown's career in Kansas are very full, and will be read with great interest."—*New Bedford Standard.*

The most exciting book of the day...... penned in that startling and graphic style which so distinguishes its talented author." — *Erie True American.*

"A spirited and graphic writer."—*Allegan Journal.*

"The book is one of intense interest."—*Montreal Transcript.*

"The book is well got up, the materials of the work well arranged by the author, and is an able tribute to old Osawatomie, who dared to beard the lion in his den to forward the object of his heart,—the liberation of the Blacks from slavery."—*Conneaut (Ohio) Reporter.*

".... Mr. Redpath loved him, and having the confidence of the family, and being with him personally much, he had abundant opportunities for learning all he wished of his life. He sympathizes with him fully. The biographer seems to have performed his task from his stand-point of view in an admirable manner.... We think it will meet the expectations which have been raised in regard to it."—*Dover (N. H.) Morning Star.*

"This is a book which will have few indorsers: for it is a thousand times more fiery than Helper's book, and glorifies John Brown throughout...... And it will find millions of readers; for Redpath is a live writer, and his reader cannot go to sleep over his pages whether he likes or dislikes the discourse. The book is equal to the greatest sensation-story in interest; and then the truth is stranger than fiction."—*Portsmouth (N. H.) Morning Chronicle.*

"A very interesting book."—*Haverhill (Mass.) Gazette.*

"An interesting, and we doubt not a truthful history of one of the most remarkable men of the age."—*Hallowell (Me.) Gazette.*

"A very earnest and hearty vindication of the life and character of the hero of Harper's Ferry, and, at the same time, a minute and accurate history of his public career."—*Lynn Reporter.*

"The author, James Redpath, was peculiarly qualified to undertake the task, and has produced a book which is at once truthful, reliable, and interesting, and which will go far toward redeeming the old man's memory from the oblcquy attempted to be cast upon it by the violent upholders and justifiers of the slave-power." — *Lancaster (Pa.) Examiner and Herald.*

"There are few books that have so large a sale, and perhaps so few indorsers. It is a sensation-book throughout; full of both blood and thunder." —*Boston Temperance Visitor.*

"Mr. Redpath has brought to this 'labor of love' literary attainments of a high order, the advantage of an intimate personal acquaintance with the distinguished subject, and thorough devotion to the cause which was nearest the heart of the old captain. He has besides had possession of numerous unpublished letters and manuscripts of old Brown, and enjoyed the confidence and assistance of his family. The book is a noteworthy contribution to literature."—*Prarie du Chien Leader.*

"The book is graphically written."—*Amherst (N. H.) Farmer's Cabinet.*

"A faithful biography of the veteran, by one who is eminently qualified, by ability and inclination, to do his memory justice." — *Cape Cod Advocate.*

"Every reading man in Kansas knows that James Redpath is an able historian, one peculiarly qualified to write the life of John Brown."—*Leavenworth Daily State Register.*

"Full of the fanaticism that led its subject to the scaffold."— *N. Y. Express.*

"A well-executed narrative of Brown's public life, by a man eminently qualified, both by personal knowledge and literary ability, for the task."—*Chicopee (Mass.) Journal.*

"Well written."—*Groton R. R. Mercury.*

"Written in Redpath's nervous and graphic style."—*Freedom's Champion (Kansas).*

"Rather an interesting work."—*Nunda (N. Y.) News.*

"Mr. Redpath knew John Brown in Kansas, and does full justice to his glorious and heroic achievements there."—*Yates Co. Chronicle.*

"Truthful and reliable and full of interest."—*Manheim (Pa.) Sentinel.*

"The letter in which the old man records his own recollections of his boyhood, is as charming for its simplicity and truthfulness, as anything in the autobiography of Benjamin Franklin, and no one can read it without seeing in it a revelation of those qualities which have made the author the remarkable man he was."—*Bloomsburg (Pa.) Republican.*

"It contains a full and interesting life of the old hero,—the representative man of the 19th century."—*Ware (Mass.) Standard.*

"This book is at present having a very extensive circulation, and, judging from the terseness and pungency with which it is written, together with the well-known ability of the author as a writer, we predict that its circulation will for a long time continue to increase rather than diminish. It contains a fine steel engraving of Captain Brown, and will be read with interest by thousands, not among the immediate partisans of the writer and his subject."—*South Reading Gazette.*

"Redpath was the companion of Brown in Kansas, and everybody knows the trip-hammer eloquence of his style in the historical descriptive. Capt. Brown's life is full of romance, and he was unquestionably a man of heart as well as head. The portion of Kansas history contained in this book is valuable."—*Boston Christian Freeman.*

"The published life of John Brown by Redpath, proves conclusively that he had been a monomaniac on the Slavery question for twenty years, and that he was not a Republican in party bias or action, but acted contrary to Republican views, and in opposition to the earnest wishes of his personal friends in the Republican ranks." — *Lewisburg (Pa.) Star and Chronicle.*

"Mr. Redpath has collected with diligence and patience, the material necessary for forming an accurate biography. To the general public, as well as to those who sympathized with John Brown, the book will possess much interest. It gives all desirable information in regard to its hero, from his boyhood up to the time of his execution." — *Boston Evening Gazette.*

"The well-known James Redpath is an Abolitionist of the darkest hue, and upholds every action of Brown. The book can do no harm."—*Montgomery Democrat.*

"We can recommend it as a very full and good account of the renowned hero..... He has succeeded in producing a book of varied interest." — *Spiritual Age.*

"John Brown reminds us of old Cromwell; for like him, he trusted in the Lord and kept his powder dry. He had great piety, good fighting qualities, and unflinching courage, as Mr. Redpath conclusively proves in his entertaining book."—*Boston Investigator.*

"It is a live book from a fearless pen."—*Fulton (Pa.) Republican.*

"It is written by one of the very few whose sympathy has extended even to an unqualified indorsement of his scheme. There is much in the book which we think unwise and cannot approve; yet it is written with great sincerity and honesty of purpose, and has all the well-known force, point, and vigor of the author's style."—*Boston Christian Register.*

"Redpath is one of the best descriptive writers of the present day."—*Westfield News Letter.*

"No unprejudiced man or woman can rise from a perusal of the book without being convinced that however fanatical they may consider him, yet that *he* considered that he was doing as he would be done by, in obedience to the commands of his Lord and Master, and that he was anything but the bloodthirsty man the slaveocracy of the land would fain make the world believe."—*Calais (Maine) Advertiser.*

"Mr. Redpath, the author of this book, was in Kansas during the exciting scenes of 1856 and 1857, employed as the special correspondent of the St. Louis *Democrat,* and his pungent and graphic letters to that journal attracted general attention. Here he first encountered John Brown; and here, perhaps, he acquired much of that spirit which now makes him an open advocate and adviser of slave insurrection.

"Since that period, he has been the warm friend and enthusiastic admirer of the subject of his biography. In a Free State Convention, held in Kansas two years ago, to consider the propriety of voting for State officers under the Lecompton Constitution, (that the friends of freedom, having possession of all the offices under that infamous instrument, might the more effectually crush it,) Mr. Redpath advocated the election of old John Brown to the governorship, that the Border Ruffians might understand what the Free-State men meant, by voting under their attempted usurpation! More than a year later, Mr. Redpath published a very radical anti-slavery work; he dedicated it to John Brown.

"Writing the present volume (under the sanction of the widow and children of the deceased) was to him, therefore, a labor of love. He believes in John Brown first, last, and always; and has no words for him but those of the most unqualified laudation.

"He criticises the Republican as bitterly as the Democrat; has little charity for those who believe that the ballot-box is the proper agency for the removal of slavery; and not only admires the character of his hero, for its constant courage, its grand unselfishness, and its simple trust in God; but also claims that all his public acts were judicious, prudent, and right.

"Writing from this point of view, he has naturally fallen into a fatal hero-worship, and often fails in exercising a just discrimination.

"He wields, however, a facile pen; and has produced a work, which, not only from the intrinsic interest of the subject, but also from its spirited and graphic style, must obtain a wide circulation."—*Boston Congregationalist.*

"In the present state of political feeling, only a limited class can look impartially on the life of John Brown. On the one hand, he is extolled and sanctified; on the other, vilified and blackened without limit.

"Yet, with all this excited partisan feeling, there are few who could read this biography without being attracted and interested in the displays of independence of thought, energy of action, probity, industry, and self-consecration to a perhaps arbitrary standard of duty with which it is filled.

"It is eminently a biography of facts, and as such possesses interest The author heartily indorses every act of John Brown. There are comparatively few who go so far as that; but no one, we think, can read the memoir without being impressed with the conviction that he was an honest and remarkable man."—*Boston Journal.*

"The accurate compilation of the facts, in this life of John Brown, shows to poor advantage by the side of the bitter spirit the editor betrays toward, not merely slaveholders, but all men whose opinions are not his own; rather the contrary.

"And his blind hero-worship, we should say, only made him still less qualified to be a just and entirely useful biographer.

"In a proper and effective biography, there should be no taking of sides, — no signs of anything like partisanship,—not the least disposition to make out a case! if there is, the real and permanent value of the performance is to that extent impaired.

"And this should be our general criticism of the author of the present volume, who has, nevertheless, put his whole heart into his work."—*Banner of Light.*

"The spirit in which such a work as this must be written, is very fairly indicated in the matter and manner of the dedication, which is to Wendell Phillips, Ralph Waldo Emerson, and Henry D. Thoreau, under the title of 'Defenders of the faithful, who, when the mob shouted madman! said saint.'

"The point of view from which that man must write of the life and actions of John Brown, who could call him 'saint,' and attempt to prove his title to that appellation, may be easily understood; and, consequently, while the book will fulfil the ardent aspirations of those who regard the hero of the Charlestown insurrection as a martyr, it will mislead no one else, nor aid in any considerable degree in inducing future ages to believe him any such wronged and suffering individual. Neither Mr. James Redpath, nor yet the chivalry of Virginia, are the men who can measure John Brown for the appreciation of future ages, if any such things, there may be with sufficient heed for the doings of to-day to speak of them. 'Madman' he was not, nor yet exactly 'saint.' 'Fanatic,' he was, of the hardest and least manageable type, with stubborn bravery and endurance to bear him on, and just enough uneducated to make him dangerous......

"The gallows, in these days, is getting to be a pretty sure precursor of immortality, and a place upon library book-shelves. John Brown has taken his turn at the one, and Redpath starts him on his career of the other. That he has done so energetically, nervously, and with a goodly array of really interesting facts, to make more generally acceptable a book which could otherwise only have found a sectional circle of readers,—there can be no question.

"The public history of John Brown will be canonized on Cornhill, and furnish texts for innumerable lamentations from the Cheeverian pulpit over this degenerate and evil age. We are quite willing to accord to it a full measure of ability, while we lack words to express the contempt which is inevitable for the whining tone of comparison which runs through the whole book, between the Baresark fanatic of Harper's Ferry and the worthies of every portion of Scripture record which can be dragged into service.—*New York Leader*.

"Mr. Redpath is a friend in need, and comes up like a trump to the defence of old Osawatomie Brown, at a time when his aid is most required to shield the old man's reputation from the attacks of even his professed friends. The great multitude have decided that John Brown was an honest fanatic and enthusiast, whose enthusiasm amounted to the frenzy of madness. But Mr. Redpath does not consider him anything of the kind. On the contrary, he considers his hero as a cool-headed saint, who accidentally failed to accomplish his great work.

"Whatever may be thought of old Brown and his biographer, whether they be regarded as saints and heroes, or fools or fanatics, all will agree that the book is an extremely interesting one, and that Mr. Redpath, in the brief space allowed him, has done wonders in constructing so interesting a narrative of the events of the remarkable man whose mad pranks have convulsed these States as they have never been convulsed before. Mr. Redpath completed his work just in time to escape from the arm of the law which was extended towards him, for the purpose of extracting from him some facts in relation to the conspiracy against the State of Virginia. As Mr. Redpath knew more than any other man on this subject, it is a great pity he could not have been prevailed upon to enlighten Congress on the subject."—*N. Y. Courier*.

"This is a complete life of 'John Brown, of Osawatomie.' It is well and candidly written, by one of his most ardent admirers; and as a history of one of the most daring, and, at the same time, one of the most infatuated men of the age, it is complete. From the first to the last page, it is full of stirring incidents; and, presenting a clear history of the Kansas struggle and Brown's connection therewith, makes it a valuable acquisition to the history of the times."—*Independent Banner*.

"The work is written well, with the exception of being highly colored in some portions."—*Home Gazette*.

"In the book before us, we have his whole history, from his childhood to his honored grave, written by a master hand. Mr. Redpath was a warm, personal friend of the glorious old hero."—*Frederick Douglass' Paper*.

"This work contains the materials for the true life of the new Peter the Hermit, who sought to redeem the Holy Places of Humanity.

"This Life must be written from a philosophic stand-point, co-ordinate in elevation to Brown's intent, and must not justify to Gideon and Samuel and the other model barbarians, whom we venerate at a distance of five thousand years, but would imprison for life in any civilized community. John Brown's method of dealing with slavery was a piece with his false theology, and his uncultured mind; his virtue, his fidelity, are what makes the world fit to live in.

"Look not at the arrow, but the mark; so shall you read from these absorbing incidents, a life which Mr. Redpath, with his honest but coarse pencil, can portray.

"A friend has handed us the following, which we give in lieu of a more detailed account of this intensely interesting book." —*Dial, Cincinnati, Ohio.*

"It would have been well if this book had never been written. Mr. Redpath has understood neither the opportunities opened to him, nor the responsibilities laid upon him, in being permitted to write the authorized life of John Brown. This book, in whatever light it is viewed, whether as the biography of a remarkable man, as a historic narrative of a series of extraordinary and important events, or simply as a piece of mere literary job-work, is equally unsatisfactory. He has shown himself incompetent to appreciate the character of the man whom he admires, and he has consequently done great wrong to his memory.... Its tone is such, it is so extravagant, that it will offend all right-thinking men.... This book is written in the spirit and style of an abolition tract.... The most interesting and the most novel part of Mr. Redpath's book is the letter written by John Brown in 1857, giving some account of his early life. It is in all respects a remarkable composition.... That John Brown was wrong in his attempt to break up slavery by violence, few will deny."—*Professor Norton, in the Atlantic Monthly.*

"The *Atlantic Monthly*, in a critical notice of Redpath's Memoir of John Brown, says: 'It reads like an abolition tract.' I believe the book is worthy of this praise. It gives us, in a style of great simplicity and directness, a narrative of highly important facts, and of that condition of manners and morals, that depravity in Church and State, which gave birth to them. It is a great and rare advantage to have a book (which must inevitably be so widely read as this) entirely free from the detestable cant which is popularly written and read in regard to slavery; the assumption of the church, that the holding of men and women as property is approved by God, and compatible with Christianity; of the State, that this is a practice which may properly be enforced by a white majority against a black minority; of the Republicans, that, however bad North of Mason and Dixon's line, slavery is sacred and inviolable South of it; of the merchants, that trade is of more consequence than human rights; of the literary class, that Southern gentlemen and scholars ought not to be interfered with, merely for the sake of ignorant and stupid people, black or white; and of the mass of unreflecting men and women, that whatever is established is, of course, to be supported and perpetuated. It is much, I say, to have a popular book, free from these enormous and pernicious public errors.

"But the merit of Mr. Redpath's book is not merely of this negative kind.

"It teaches, by implication, positively just and right sentiments upon the momentous subject of slavery. It everywhere takes for granted these great truths,—that slavery, except for the sake of crime, is itself a crime; that the relation of slaveholder to slave gives no rights to the former, and imposes no obligation upon the latter; that freedom is the right of every slave, and that his duty and interest alike call upon him to assume this right whenever practicable; that humanity and Christianity alike require the interference of others for the help of the slave, whenever and wherever such help can be made available; that it is owing to the corruption of manners and morals, naturally engendered by a slaveholding Church and State, and by the labors of clergymen and legislators in behalf of slavery, that so little active interference in aid of the slaves has yet been attempted; that it is becoming more and more manifest that such interference is demanded, not only for the help of the slaves, but to prevent the rights of white citizens of the North being entirely swallowed up by the increasing incursions of the slave-power, and that it should be remembered, whenever slaves are aided on the soil, where they have spent their lives in enforced labor without wages, *that, as a general rule*, the movable property found in the possession of the slaveholder, rightfully belongs to the slave, and may properly be used, by himself or his agent, in his service.

"Being thus free from the prejudices naturally existing among the less intelligent people in a slaveholding nation, (because directly fostered and perpetuated by their leaders in Church and State,) and being founded on a high morality and a pure religion, the laws of justice and of love, this book possesses the further resemblance to 'an abolition tract,' that it takes the stand-point which history, the judgment of the wise and good, and (after these) popular opinion itself, must ultimately take. After slavery shall have been abolished, the flimsy defences now patched up for it by priests and politicians will utterly disappear; the arguments of abolitionists, now called fanatical by slaveholders and their Northern tools, will appear manifest truisms, the obvious voice of common sense, humanity, justice, and religion, and the wonder will be that a popular opinion and a national custom, adverse to them, could have existed in the nineteenth century, after the declaration, by the ancestors of that same people, in the eighteenth, that the inalienable freedom of all men was a self-evident truth.

"When we know, in addition to the above, that Mr. Redpath's book possesses the quality (not enjoyed by all 'abolition tracts') of being extremely interesting, and that it finds, in consequence, an extensive sale and an increasing number of readers, we may hope that it will sow the seeds of many enterprises for the help of the slave, and waken many hearts to inquire what they can do, directly as well as indirectly, in his behalf."—*C. K. Whipple in the Boston Liberator.*

"The author seems to have done the man justice......It exhibits him as a man, a Christian, doing what he believed to be right,—a *working* rather than a *theoretical* philanthropist....This book is valuable for reference in relation to the disgraceful and bloody scenes which took place in Kansas, during the conflict between slavery and freedom in that distracted territory."—*Lincoln (Maine) Advertiser.*

"Redpath is a violent abolitionist, and believes that Brown's conduct was justifiable and renders him a hero and a saint. He writes in intense admiration of Brown, and of course uses his best endeavors to convince his readers of the glorious character of his mode. There are very many who will not like this book upon that account. It is too highly colored, and will have to be read with caution, so that it will be necessary to weigh all the statements made, and separate extravagant eulogy from fact."—*Philadelphia Sunday Dispatch.*

"Mr. Redpath was just the man to write this biography, having a strong sympathy with the subject, and being conversant with the events which had been the occasion of this character's development.... We have read the book, and we believe thousands will read it, with pleasure and profit. It is the most refreshing draught we have taken from the well of our English literature for a long time. It is evident that the writer loves his subject as a brother, and admires him as a hero; but we find no fault with this, for we cannot help loving and admiring him, too. If there are a few more such true souls as his left in our country, she is rich indeed. The account incorporated into this work of the family of John Brown, at North Elba, written by T. W. Higginson, is one of the most touching things we ever read. The story of his camp life and battles in Kansas, is full of the highest romance, and reveals the actor as a hero of magnificent proportions."—*East Boston Ledger.*

"An able history of an eventful and unusually stirring and active life."—*New York Waverley.*

II.

ECHOES OF HARPER'S FERRY. Edited by JAMES REDPATH, and Dedicated to His Excellency Fabre Geffrard, President of the Republic of Hayti. Boston: Thayer & Eldridge, 114 & 116 Washington Street. 1860. pp. 514. Price $1.25. Sent by mail, prepaid, on receipt of the retail price.

This volume is a collection of the greatest Speeches, Sermons, Lectures, Letters, Poems, and other Utterances of the leading minds of America and Europe, called forth by John Brown's Invasion of Virginia. They are all given — mostly for the first time — *unabridged;* and they have all been corrected by their authors for this edition, or reprinted with their permission from duly authorized copies. That this volume is justly entitled to the claim for being the *first* collection of worthy specimens of American Eloquence, the following summary of its contents will show.

It contains revised and unabridged *Speeches, Discourses, Sermons,* and *Lectures,* by Wendell Phillips (2), Ralph Waldo Emerson (2), Henry D. Thoreau, Edward Everett, Henry Ward Beecher, Charles O'Conor, Rev. Gilbert Haven, Rev. Edwin M. Wheelock, Dr. Cheever (2), Fales Henry Newhall, Theodore Tilton, William A. Phillips, Rev. M. D. Conway, Rev. James Freeman Clarke; *Letters* and *Essays* by Victor Hugo (2), Theodore Parker (2,) Lydia M. Child and Mrs. Mason of Virginia, Wm. Lloyd Garrison, John G. Whittier, Elizur Wright, &c. &c.; brief contributions from C. K. Whipple, Hon. Mr. Tilden, Rev. Mr. Belcher, Richard Realf, &c.; *Poems* by Wm. Allinghame, Rev. E. H. Sears, L. M. Alcott, Mrs. Child, Wm. D. Howells, F. B. Sanborn, &c.

Annexed to these various productions are the autographs of their authors — Phillips, Emerson, Thoreau, Alcott, Parker, John Brown, Sears, Tilton, Wm. Phillips, Cheever, Newhall, Haven, Everett, Beecher, O'Conor, Whittier, Garrison, Whipple, Conway, Tilden, &c.

The *Appendix* contains the widely celebrated statistical articles of Henry C. Carey, of Philadelphia, on the *Value of the Union to the North;* a series of essays (covering 60 pages of small type in the volume) which may safely be recommended as a specific to the "business interests of the country," whenever that respectable body is again threatened with an attack of Union-saving.

This collection received the same style of praise and of censure which greeted the appearance of the Life of John Brown. It is therefore unnecessary to give specimens of either.

III.

SOUTHERN NOTES FOR NATIONAL CIRCULATION. Edited by JAMES REDPATH. Boston: Thayer & Eldridge, 114 and 116 Washington Street. A handsome pamphlet of 132 pages. Price 25 cents.

This is a volume of *facts* of recent Southern life, as narrated by the Southern and Metropolitan press. It is not too much to say that, next to Charles Sumner's Speech, it is the most unanswerable and exhaustive impeachment of the Slave Power that has hitherto been published. Although treating of different topics, it extends, completes, and strengthens the argument of the Senator. It is a history of the Southern States for six months subsequent to John Brown's Invasion of Virginia. No one who has read Sumner's Speech should fail to procure this pamphlet. The diversity of its contents may be judged from the titles of its Chapters — Key Notes, Free Speech South, Free Press South, Law of the Suspected, Southern Gospel Freedom, Southern Hospitality, Post Office South, Our Adopted Fellow-Citizens South, Persecutions of Southern Citizens, The Shivering Chivalry, Sports of Heathen Gentlemen. As a manual for Anti-Slavery and Republican orators and editors it is invaluable.

www.ingramcontent.com/pod-product-compliance
Lightning Source LLC
LaVergne TN
LVHW011224110826
845150LV00006B/1541